T0271411

The Logistics Audit

Extraordinary technological progress, but also the experience gained from the global COVID-19 pandemic, force the future vision of the world's economic development to assume a close coexistence and intense interaction between production (manufacturing) and logistics and supply-chain management. This perspective requires that the current functioning of organizations will have to be radically remodeled so that they can face not only market competition but also the turbulent changes (volatility, uncertainty, complexity, and ambiguity - VUCA) that take place in their close environment. Therefore, in the next few years, one of the most important tools for improving organizations may become industry audits, especially the logistics audit.

This book explores the development, methods, and impact of logistics audits on organizations. In a holistic way, the book refers to topics such as internal audit, control, logistics system of enterprises, principles of conducting logistics audit and its problem areas (risk), logistics audit of procurement, production, warehousing, distribution, and supply chains, impact of the digital economy on organizations, and the European market for logistics audit services. Undoubtedly, the greatest asset of this book is that, in international terms, it is the first compact book devoted to the issue of logistics audit.

Unique and timely, the book will be an essential resource for academics and postgraduate students of logistics, supply-chain management, and global operations in particular.

Piotr Buła is an Associate Professor and Head of the International Management Department at Krakow University of Economics (KUE), Poland, Vice-Rector for Projects and Cooperation (KUE), former Director of Cracow School of Business (CUE), Senior Research Professor in Business Management Department at the University of Johannesburg, South Africa, and Grand Valley State University scholarship holder. He is the author or co-author of more than 175 publications in economics and management. His research interests focus on aspects related to the application of artificial intelligence and neuromanagement, risk management, internal audit, international management, and logistics. A member of international organizations associating professors and business practitioners in the management area: EFMD, CEEMAN, IMDA, GBATA, EIBA, GSSI, IAMB, EECSA, SAIMS.

Bartosz Niedzielski is an Assistant Professor at Krakow University of Economics, Poland. He studied and conducted scientific activities, among other subjects, at the University of Greenwich (UK), University of Oxford (UK), London School of Economics (UK), Deggendorf Institute of Technology (DE), and Jagiellonian University (PL). He has over ten years of professional experience gained in global corporations in the BPO/SCC sector (mainly at HSBC). His research interests focus on aspects related to the application of artificial intelligence in organizations, management, and internal audit. He is the author or co-author of more than 50 scientific publications in economics and management, including the monograph entitled *Management, Organizations and Artificial Intelligence: Where Theory Meets Practice* (Routledge, 2021).

Routledge Focus on Business and Management

The fields of business and management have grown exponentially as areas of research and education. This growth presents challenges for readers trying to keep up with the latest important insights. *Routledge Focus on Business and Management* presents small books on big topics and how they intersect with the world of business research.

Individually, each title in the series provides coverage of a key academic topic, whilst collectively, the series forms a comprehensive collection across the business disciplines.

Systems Thinking and Sustainable Healthcare Delivery
Ben Fong

Gender Diversity and Inclusion at Work
Divergent Views from Turkey
Zeynep Özsoy, Mustafa Şenyücel and Beyza Oba

Management and Visualisation
Seeing Beyond the Strategic
Gordon Fletcher

Knowledge Management and AI in Society 5.0
Manlio Del Giudice, Veronica Scuotto and Armando Papa

The Logistics Audit
Methods, Organization, and Practice
Piotr Buła and Bartosz Niedzielski

For more information about this series, please visit: www.routledge.com/
Routledge-Focus-on-Business-and-Management/book-series/FBM

The Logistics Audit
Methods, Organization, and Practice

Piotr Buła and Bartosz Niedzielski

LONDON AND NEW YORK

First published 2023
by Routledge
4 Park Square, Milton Park, Abingdon, Oxon OX14 4RN

and by Routledge
605 Third Avenue, New York, NY 10158

Routledge is an imprint of the Taylor & Francis Group, an informa business

British Library Cataloguing-in-Publication Data
A catalogue record for this book is available from the British Library

ISBN: 978-1-032-46126-7 (hbk)
ISBN: 978-1-032-46127-4 (pbk)
ISBN: 978-1-003-38018-4 (ebk)

DOI: 10.4324/9781003380184

Typeset in Times New Roman
by Deanta Global Publishing Services, Chennai, India

Contents

Acknowledgments

We had no doubt that attempting to integrate the knowledge of audit and logistics scattered throughout the literature would be both a demanding and an inspiring endeavor. The biggest challenge was the fact that both subdisciplines of management and quality sciences draw on a number of other academic specialties, notably economics, finance, and praxeology. The limitations adopted in the course of research allowed us to focus primarily on logistics audit as a comprehensive technique and independent diagnostic tool of company logistics systems.

In doing so, we have set a new research direction that may prove useful for future explorations in logistics audit and all its components, from procurement to distribution − a fact that was also noted by the book's reviewers, for which we are extremely grateful. With this in mind, we, as authors, believe that the book has met or will meet its objectives, which include, first and foremost, an attempt to organize and supplement existing knowledge on logistics audit in the broader context of other types of audit and, secondly, to prepare a compact publication that will provide a wide audience with a basic reference on logistics audit and related topics.

We would like to take this opportunity to express our gratitude to all the wonderful people we met while researching and writing the book, people who made it possible. First, we would like to thank the students of International Logistics at our university, who were the moving spirit behind the entire undertaking. It was their enthusiasm and willingness to deepen their knowledge and improve their skills that started us working. We would also like to express our thanks to the authorities of the Krakow University of Economics, whose organizational and financial support turned out to be necessary almost at every stage of the implementation of this project. We are especially grateful to Anna Chrabąszcz, who acted as the managing editor and coordinator of the publishing process. Her commitment, efficiency, and editorial conscientiousness will remain in our grateful memory for a long time. It is impossible not to mention Alex Atkinson and her team at

Routledge, whose professionalism, to quote Kevin Powers, "was character-ised by a certain evolutionary beauty." The authors would also like to thank the anonymous reviewers for their time and effort, which will always be an important element of science. Finally, special thanks go to our loved ones, who have been with us at every stage of the writing process and who often understand us better than we understand ourselves.

Piotr Buła and Bartosz Niedzielski

Introduction

Today, as never before, organizations must constantly evolve and quickly adapt to the changing environment around them. This situation requires them to regularly face several challenges, whose level of intensity varies and is the result of both the external and internal environment of the organization. Most often these challenges concern aspects related to business, legal, regulatory, technological requirements, or – increasingly often – security, which, due to the rapidly growing number and size of cyberattacks in the world,[1] has now become more important than freedom itself. Nevertheless, what most determines the compulsion to change the current way of functioning of the organization and its business model are technological megatrends. In practice, they reshape reality in the economic, social, legal, and political dimensions of every contemporary organization. And although the power of influence that global technological trends have on the economies of many countries may vary, it is experienced to a greater or lesser extent by practically everyone. Technological novelties in the form of artificial intelligence, blockchain, drones, Internet of Things, robots, and virtual reality reach both poor and rich countries, large and small organizations, developed and underdeveloped nations, less and more educated societies, all religions, and both America and Africa. Thanks to these circumstances, the flat world theory, formulated by Thomas Friedman at the dawn of the 21st century, is gaining in importance and at the same time underscores that the limitations, barriers, and boundaries for innovative technologies are not confirmed – in the physical sense – in the reality that surrounds us.

Considering the above, it is impossible not to notice that the permanent turbulence of the environment generates constant pressure on the management of the organization, especially in relation to the need to achieve the strategic goals set before it. However, when taking into account the dynamics of globalization processes, the intensification of competition activities, the growing importance of risk and uncertainty in the world, as well as

DOI: 10.4324/9781003380184-1

the forces driving the development of digitization, the achievement of such goals will not be possible without the organization having specific knowledge, experience, meta-skills, qualified specialists, and tools. All of these elements must evolve on par with the changing environment so that they can productively serve the leadership in managing the entire organization. An important role in this process will probably be played by internal audits in general, and industry audits in particular. These are tools whose inherent feature is to help organizations achieve their fundamental goals. And because data, technology, and management tools are currently intertwined in almost every aspect of the functioning of the organization, this situation will also force the audit to change its current form and mode of implementation. To put it simply, there will be a transition – most likely within the next decade – from a fourth-generation audit to a fifth-generation one, which will be performed more often than before in remote form and using digital technologies. This probability entitles us to put forward the thesis that audits of the future will be digital audits. But, due to the current challenges faced by organizations, including the dynamic development of the digital economy or the still unflagging popularity of logistics – exemplified by the flourishing of the logistics services market in Poland, Europe, and beyond – a deeper look at management aspects is also needed, in the context of the logistics audit itself. Its development, as an industry audit, took place at the beginning of the 1990s, while the increase in popularity fell at the beginning of the 21st century. This makes the logistics audit, as a comprehensive and independent tool for assessing the company's logistics system, a relatively young concept, in contrast to the history of audit itself, which is over 70 years old. Consequently, management science literature – apart from definitional approaches – has not seen any wider studies and publications (including books or scientific monographs) that would satisfactorily deal with the essence, scope, and complexity of this issue. This applies to publications in English, Polish, and other languages. In addition, logistic audit terms formulated mostly in articles and industry reports, have often been and still are built using vague terms, which in practice leads to the generation of an excessive number of definitions of this concept in the scientific and journalistic literature, and consequently to terminological chaos. What's more, it is also worth noting that the elements, threads, thoughts, or problems discussed in the literature regarding the logistics audit often remain without verification or evaluation regarding the degree of their impact on management theories. Meanwhile, and this should not be forgotten, progress in science is possible thanks to the critical juxtaposing of observed things with the current state of knowledge, including strictly theoretical knowledge. It is therefore possible to identify in management sciences the existence of a certain gap in the issues devoted to the logistics audit, and, through this book, an attempt was made to create a publication whose content, layout, and richness of the presented approaches contribute to the implementation of three basic goals. First, the book is an attempt to organize, supplement, and enrich the existing knowledge about the logistics audit, compared to other types of audit. Second, it is to serve as a basic source of knowledge for a wide range of recipients interested in the subject of logistics audit, including students of higher education institutions, specialists, practitioners, academic teachers, middle and senior managers, and other people who want to deepen their knowledge in this field. And third, it is intended to be a source of inspiration for scientists and researchers who will want to conduct scientific research on the theoretical and practical aspects of the development of logistics audit in organizations and in management sciences.

The book is structured around four chapters.

Chapter 1 discusses the issues of general audit, taking into account its etymological and historical perspective. An audit typology is presented along with the goals and mission it has to achieve in the context of the organization. Then, in tabular terms, the similarities and differences between external and internal audits are presented. Similar *differentia specifica* are also presented in relation to internal audit and control, due to the frequent occurrence of blurred – also in the literature – boundaries between audit and controlling. The chapter ends with a description of tasks, work standards, and the role played by the auditor in the organization from the point of view of audit implementation. In addition, the chapter is enriched with the presentation – in tabular terms – of the scope of activities performed by the auditor and his competences.

Chapter 2 is almost entirely devoted to the logistic audit methodology. At the beginning, the logistics system of the company is described in a holistic manner, taking into account the divisions to which it is subject in the literature on the topic. Next, the basic objectives of the logistics audit are presented, including the processes and problem areas that may be its subject. These explanations are firmly embedded in the context of considerations regarding the so-called industry audits, which in practice – but also in science – are perceived as important sources of information on the condition of a given unit. In addition, an important part of this chapter is the description of the basic stages of logistics audit implementation, which are also presented in tabular form, while the procedure for its conduct is presented in graphical form. The final part of the chapter concerns the impact of the Fourth Industrial Revolution (Industry 4.0) on the changes taking place in auditing, especially in relation to the goals set for it, the style of implementation of audit tasks, the set of tools and technologies used, and the identification of places related to the accumulation of the greatest risk.

Chapter 3 presents a modular approach to logistics auditing, presenting the most well-known types, divided into: logistics audit of procurement, logistics audit of production, logistics audit of the warehouse, logistics audit of distribution, and, lastly, logistics audit of the supply chain.

Chapter 4 is more managerial in nature and focuses on two basic aspects. Firstly, it presents tools (indicators) that in practice can be used to analyze the potential of the company's logistics system and defines the risks occurring in the logistics system of the organization. Secondly, it presents a brief analysis of the development of the logistics audit services market in the national dimension, also in relation to the changes that are taking place in the market in the context of the progressing phenomenon of digitization.

Each of the chapters ends with a set of prepared control and analytical questions, whose task is to verify knowledge about the issues raised and stimulate readers to intellectual effort related to critical thinking, the final "product" of which will be the evaluation of the content read.

At the end of this introduction, the authors express the hope that the book will meet the expectations that are placed on it. To a large extent, they concern the fact that, for each of the readers, it becomes a useful item in deepening knowledge about management in general and logistics auditing in particular. May the lesson of this book be a source of development of their own talents and interests for all.

Piotr Buła and Bartosz Niedzielski

Note

1 As an example, it is worth quoting events that occurred only in the first half of 2020. The first of them was associated with the loss of USD 2.3 million by Manor Independent School District in Texas (USA), a public school system that fell victim to a successful phishing campaign carried out by cybercriminals. Then, in less than a month, the American cosmetic giant Estée Lauder, leaked onto the Internet nearly 440 million of its internal records as a result of cybercriminal activities and software security errors. Another incident concerned the Marriott hotel chain, which, as a result of cybercriminal actions, shared the data of about 5.2 million hotel guests. The last situation described here was the need for the University of California to pay a ransom of USD 1.14 million to hackers in June 2020 in order to save its ongoing research on the SARS-CoV-2 (COVID-19) acute respiratory virus.

1 Audit

A theoretical approach

1.1. Audit – definitions, types, objectives, mission

The etymology of the word "audit" dates to distant times and the Latin language, where the terms *auditare* or *audire* meant "to listen" and "to hear" respectively. At the initial stage of the development of the audit, it was indeed the case that it was the auditor who listened carefully to the numbers and bills that were provided to them, i.e., read or dictated, by the accountant. The purpose of such activity was to check the correctness of the numerical records included in the accounts, which reflected settlements of investments or trade between merchants carried out at that time. Thus, audit was a conceptual category that was already known and applied – albeit in a different content and form than is now the case – in all ancient countries, including Mesopotamia, Egypt, Greece, and Rome. Nevertheless, the heyday of auditing came with the expansion of the economic crisis that befell the United States in 1929.[1] Its consequences – both for the United States and for a large part of the world at that time – turned out to be so serious that they initiated a global discussion on the possibility of using audit as a tool to prevent similar economic anomalies in the future.

Until modern times, the concept of audit has received many definitional approaches, which is the result both of the great interest the authors take in it and of the different perspectives with which they approach research on this complex and difficult matter. One of the most general definitions of an audit, provided by Petrascu (2010), describes it as a synthetic process of independent acquisition and evaluation of information, the purpose of which is to assess the degree of its compliance with pre-established criteria and then communicate the results of this work to the interested parties of the process. The concept of auditing is similarly defined by the international Association of Chartered Certified Accountants (ACCA).[2] This group also identifies audit with the process of collecting and analyzing data, in a predefined context, whose task is to identify facts (evidence) related to a specific

DOI: 10.4324/9781003380184-2

dispute and provide preventive advice in a specific area. The disputes mentioned in this definition may take on a different nature and relate to irregularities in legal, financial, or ethical aspects. A more descriptive and narrow character of this concept is presented by Gary and Mason (2008), who argue that audit is an activity related to the investigation or search for evidence, which makes it possible to form an opinion on the veracity and reliability of the financial or other information held by a person or persons not directly related to (independent of) a given case. Thanks to this approach, the information obtained during auditing tasks is characterized by greater credibility and usefulness. In the context of the presented definitions of auditing, which by no means exhaust the richness present in subject literature, one can distinguish some general features, which concern the fact that:

- audit is a process[3] aimed at collecting, processing (analyzing), and evaluating information, in order to obtain reasonable assurance as to its compliance and reliability with specific criteria,
- audit, although most often identified within financial and accounting issues, may also concern legal, organizational, moral, or ethical matters,
- audit is a deliberate action to determine the facts, including those resulting from the accounting records, reports, procedures, or strategies of a given organization,
- audit is an independent activity,
- audit is a preventive activity,
- audit is an advisory activity aimed at formulating recommendations and recommendations that should be implemented in the reports prepared by the auditor.

In theoretical and practical terms, the audit may take various forms and types, which are determined by the scope of the adopted criterion. Pająk (2008), taking as criteria the subject of the audit, its level, scope, scope, and stage of research in this area, provides a typology, presented in Table 1.1.

The types of audits presented in Table 1.1, which can be conventionally treated as the basic and most used ones, do not exhaust the long list that has been developed over many years in this field. In practice, it was created by the scientific community researching this area as well as by organizations or individuals who carried out several audit tasks in various areas of life. As an example, it is worth mentioning other types of audits that are referred to by Costello (2003), such as compliance audit, effectiveness and performance audit, legal audit, or contract audit or by Jenkins (1992), who writes about the audit of industrial premises, site contamination audit, or audit of the impact of pollution on the environment. In recent years, popularity has increased for the latter types of audits, which can be described as

Table 1.1 Typology of audits

Criterion	Type
Audit entity	External audit
	Internal audit
Audit subject	Research and development audit
	Financial audit
	Logistic audit
	Marketing audit
	Personnel audit
	Production audit
Audit level	Strategic audit
	Operational audit
Audit scope	Organizational structure audit
	Process audit
	Organizational culture audit
	Audit of results
Audit coverage	Audit of the company
	Audit of the organization's basic subsystems
	Audit of the organizational unit
	Audit of the organizational unit
	Audit of the organizational post/position
Scope of research	Preliminary audit
	Basic audit

Source: Pająk, 2008, p. 71.

environmental. This is mainly due to the global promotion of environmental priorities, which most companies have decided to use as an excellent source of competitive advantage[4] on the market. Bearing in mind the above, we can see that the number of types of audits can be unlimited, because each area of the economy or area of life can be subject to audit activity, which in turn will lead to the creation of new names for the types of audits performed. Nevertheless, practitioners (auditors) who provide audit services on a daily basis divide audit into three main categories:

- financial audit – in which accounting auditors provide opinions on financial statements in terms of their compliance with accounting rules and standards,
- compliance audit – in which auditors verify whether the subject and scope of the audit is consistent with applicable laws, adopted proce-dures, and policies,
- operational audit – in which the subject, coverage, and scope of the audit can be discretionary or arbitrary.

At this point it should be clearly emphasized that audit, as an advisory and verification activity, is not legally obligatory for all types of organizations or institutions. The catalogue of organizations, or more precisely the areas that are subject to auditing, is – in most countries – regulated by law at the level of national legislation and related regulations. This means that in the case of, for example, Polish legislation,[5] the annual financial statements of entities such as banks or joint-stock companies are subject to mandatory audit (i.e., financial audit), while other organizations are either exempt from this obligation or must meet certain conditions in employment, assets, or net income in order to be subject to it. In other words, it can be concluded that no type of audit is obligatory for any organization, unless the obligation to carry it out results from the provisions of a national law.

Audit, as a causative action aimed at influencing the wider network of socio-economic relations, has certain goals to achieve. In the majority of subject publications those goals are clearly and precisely defined. Thanks to this, stakeholders know what they can expect from conducting audit activities in each area, both in the short and long term. Table 1.2 presents core audit objectives in the context of the role assigned to it in the financial and operational sphere of the economy. At the same time, it should be remembered that these goals are subject to constant evolution (change), due to the development of business models and techniques.

Table 1.2 Core audit objectives

Objectives	Tasks
Main objective	Determination of the reliability of the presented financial and operational information, with the facts.
	Ensuring that the organization's accounts and transactions reflect its true and fair image.
	Formulation of an independent opinion on the reliability and honesty of information obtained during audit tasks.
Auxiliary objectives	Detection and prevention of fraud concerning manipulation and embezzlement of funds, falsification of financial data and so-called sensitive data, improper application and interpretation of applicable legal regulations.
	Detection and elimination of financial and operational errors.
	Identification of processes requiring improvement (improvement of efficiency).
	Assessment of compliance of the functioning of the organization and the tasks performed by it with all applicable provisions of national and/or international law.
	Determination of the effectiveness of the procedures and policies present in the organization.
	Analysis and evaluation of the scope of professional responsibility and duties specified in a given position.

Source: Authors' own study.

In addition to the objectives listed in Table 1.2, audit also has a specific mission to fulfill, which, depending on its type, may take different forms.[6] In practice, the audit mission differs from its objectives; it is not intended to achieve specific results in a given organization but to build a sense of community in thinking about audit as a tool in the area of management and finance that helps organizations and individuals to be reliable and honest partners in creating business networks valuable to the economy. And, just as ACCA's mission is to shape future leaders of the business world and to share specialist and expert knowledge, as well as to promote high professional standards, the mission of any audit should be to make the economic world better and more valuable, which can be realized through:

- supporting the management functions of organizations and institutions through continuous and multi-level evaluation,
- identification and monitoring of irregularities and emerging risks (threats) resulting from the conducted activity, and then their consistent reduction or elimination,
- initiating changes and presenting proposals for improvement, as a mechanism for self-improvement,
- the protection of employees, assets, and information, which are valuable resources for any organization.

The issues presented in this section of the chapter concerning the definition, types, objectives, and mission that audit must fulfill introduce further considerations about the logistics audit and the functions it has to fulfill in the context of a system as complex as the economy. Thanks to the conceptual instruments presented in this section, the reader can move on to further issues related to the audit, which will be characterized by an increasing degree of detail and span. The next section discusses the differences and similarities between external and internal audit, taking into account the subjective criterion of the audit (see Table 1.1).

1.2. External audit *vs.* internal audit – similarities and differences

The subjective criterion adopted in literature on the topic, in the context of the types of audits (see Table 1.1), divides audit into external and internal. It is the most well-known and cardinal division that we deal with when it comes to audit. At the outset, to understand the essence of this division, including its similarities and differences, it is necessary to define both types. One of the definitions of external audit proposed by Satka (2017) states that it is an audit that is carried out by third parties to, for example, verify the correctness of presented financial statements. At the same time – as the author quickly adds – external audit is not limited by anything, so its scope of activity may exceed the generally accepted framework. In other words, it can refer to other aspects of the organization's functioning, not necessarily related to accounting or finance. A slightly different definition is proposed by Nasta and Ladar (2015), in which they not only describe what an external audit is and what is aimed at but also what its primary duty is. According to these authors, the external audit is carried out with the help of independent and external entities and is aimed at conducting a financial analysis along with an assessment of its risk to the organization's activities. In addition, it is primarily addressed to the organization's stakeholders, to obtain reliable information on the financial situation of the company. On the other hand, the main obligation of an external audit is to conduct an annual audit of financial statements, with the purpose of issuing an opinion on the correctness or irregularity of the company's financial situation. One of the most well-known and most cited definitions of external audit is the one proposed by the Chartered Institute of Management Accountants (CIMA).[7] Representatives of this organization – in a narrow sense – define external audit as periodic audits of documentation and accounting operations of entities by a person, who is an auditor,[8] in order to maintain correctness, reliability, honesty, applicable accounting standards, and legal requirements in the image of financial statements of entities. In opposition to the definition proposed by CIMA, the one by Larcker,[9] who – in broad terms – considers external audit to be nothing more than an assessment of the importance and credibility of publicly reported financial information. At the same time – as Larcker clearly emphasizes – the management of the organization is responsible for preparing financial reports, and shareholders[10] expect only impartial information about the company, which will come from independent people. The above definitions of external audit – despite their interpretative diversity – have many common features. They mainly concern the fact that external audit is most often identified with activities that are not only independent and reliable but are, above all, related to the periodic analysis of financial statements and accounts of entities. In practice, this means that external audit is almost always identified with the financial sphere – and, more specifically, accounting – of a given organization, and less often with its operational or managerial sphere. What's more, it is an action, by a given organization (enterprise managers), aimed at fulfilling the provisions of the accounting law in force in this domain as well as the competences to reliably inform shareholders about the financial situation of the company. What is often included in the definition of an external audit is the important role to be played by the person of the auditor, i.e., an independent expert whose task is to obtain reliable information on the financial situation of the enterprise and issue an appropriate report in this respect.

Different than external auditing is the concept of an internal audit, which – especially over the last two decades[11] – has taken on both academic and functional significance. According to the definition of the Institute of Internal Auditors (IIA),[12] internal audit[13] is seen as an independent and objective activity aimed at bringing added value that improves the functioning of a specific organization. Improvement in this area is to take place by increasing the efficiency of processes, identifying and reducing risks or systematic supervision over implemented projects. An extremely concise and precise definition of this conceptual category is proposed by Montgomery (1956), who presents internal audit as an independent evaluation function established in an organization to examine and evaluate its activities. However, as Montgomery observes, internal audit is a form of advisory service provided to a specific organization, which is non-obligatory. Swinkels (2012), examining the theoretical aspects of internal audit in relation to the control systems in force in Dutch listed companies, stated that, in fact, internal audit focuses on activities certifying certain data and information, as well as on consultative work. This would mean that internal audit has – among others – an important proactive (initiating) function in relation to the client's needs, in areas related to control, management, risk, and monitoring, without losing its independence and credibility. Definitions of internal audit by other authors, including Hermanson et al. (2008), draw attention – as was the case with the definition of external audit – to the role played by internal auditors. Thanks to their qualifications in the field of management, risk management, or internal control, they work on achieving the required level of compliance with the law in force in each organization or with adopted procedures and policies. In addition to features associated with independence and objectivity of functioning, the definitions of internal audit presented above are connected by the fact that they are clearly focused on activities in the managerial and operational sphere rather than the financial sphere of the organization. Thus, internal audit is an activity that covers a much wider range of activities than an external audit. However, the number of differences between external and internal audit is much richer and is presented in Table 1.3.

In light of the presented differences between external and internal audits, one should not draw the conclusion that these are types of audits that are in competition with each other; these are areas that, particularly from the point of view of organization, complement each other and form an important aspect of the means to its improvement. Thus, both external and internal audits are important for every organization regardless of its size, scope of activity, or the industry in which it operates. What's more, the

Table 1.3 External audit versus internal audit – comparative approach

External audit	Internal audit
The purpose of an external audit is to verify the correctness of the prepared financial statements	The purpose of internal audit is to bring added value to improve the functioning of the organization
An external audit is an *ex post* audit (follow-up audit)	Internal audit is primarily an *ex ante* audit (prior audit)
An external audit is performed by people from outside the organization	Internal audit can be performed by people from the organization.
An external audit is often "incidental" and is performed once a year	Internal audit is permanent
An external audit focuses on identifying fraud and irregularities in an organization's financial statements	Internal audit focuses on identifying and preventing fraud and irregularities
External audit concerns accounting and bookkeeping activities	Internal audit concerns business and management activities
The implementation of an external audit related to the audit of accounting books is most often obligatory and results from the provisions of applicable law	The implementation of internal audit is voluntary and discretionary
External audit examines the financial aspects of business activity	Internal audit examines all aspects of business activity
External audit scope is limited	The scope of internal audit is unlimited
External audit is carried out on the basis of applicable national legislation (especially the accounting act)	Internal audit is carried out on the basis of applicable procedures and policies adopted in the organization
External audit has a limited impact on the improvement of the organization	Internal audit is the basic tool for improving an organization in all its aspects
External audit has an advisory and verification function	Internal audit has an advisory, verification, control, and proactive function
External audit focuses mainly on finance and accounting departments	Internal audit focuses on all departments in the organization, procedures, and their functions
The value provided to the organization by an external audit is the accuracy, correctness, and reliability of the prepared financial statements and the accounting books kept	The value provided to the organization by internal audit is the operational efficiency of the organization
External audit concerns the operational level in the organization	Internal audit can concern the strategic, operational, and tactical level of the organization
The auditor is elected by the board of directors (management) of the company	The auditor is elected by the management of the company or by the shareholders

(*Continued*)

Table 1.3 (Continued)

External audit	Internal audit
The external auditor does not know the organization well and gets acquainted with it during the implementation of audit tasks	The internal auditor knows the organization well – they are its employee
The external auditor has extensive experience in the implementation of audit tasks	The internal auditor may not have sufficient knowledge and experience in the performance of audit tasks
The main standards for external auditors in the course of their work are International Accounting Standards (IAS) and International Financial Reporting Standards (IFRS)	The main standards for internal auditors in the course of their work are International Standards for Professional Practice of Internal Audit, institute of Internal Auditors (IIA standards)
Auditor – statutory auditor	Auditor – internal auditor
External audit qualifications – certificates such as ACCA, CFA*	Internal audit qualifications – certificates such as CIA**, CISA***
Objectivism	The risk of lack of objectivity
High implementation costs	Low implementation costs

Source: Authors' own elaboration based on secondary research.
*Chartered Financial Analyst (CFA), ** Certified Internal Auditor (CIA), *** Certified Information Systems Auditor (CISA).

interpenetration of similarities in the context of these two types of audits can be observed on many levels, related to:

- autonomy of action – both external and internal audits are characterized by freedom of action and a high degree of independence. In practice, it boils down to the fact that the work carried out as part of each audit is free from prejudice, impartial and objective, avoiding conflicts of interest, and conducted with due diligence within the framework of applicable standards,
- objectives – the basic goal of the external and the internal audit is primarily to identify errors and detect fraud in the organization's activities,
- reporting - the results of both types of audits are formally prepared reports on their implementation in the form of post-audit reports
- planning – all stages related to the implementation of both external and internal audit are carried out in the same, clearly defined and uniform, way. Thus, everything starts with the preparation of audit plans and ends with the publication of reports after those plans have been carried out,
- testing – both financial auditors and internal auditors verify the correctness of, for example, transactions or processes using a tool such as validation (testing),

- risk – is the basic conceptual category that constantly accompanies the implementation of objectives and tasks resulting from conducting external and internal audits,
- work standards – both types of audit must be carried out at a high substantive and organizational level so that they guarantee the reliability and correctness of the results achieved. In this context, international standards of external and internal audit practice, which have been issued by professional organizations and which, in many areas, e.g., related to professional ethics, are convergent with each other.

The similarities presented above may therefore constitute a certain proof regarding the existence of complementarity in the relationship between external and internal audit. Its practical application – especially in the context of improving the effectiveness and quality of operation – could primarily benefit the entire organization because, as Pop et al. (2008) rightly point out:

- internal audit is complementary to external audit, because in organizations where internal audit has already been implemented, external audit is more determined to appreciate, in a different manner, the correct and reliable view of financial results and reports,
- external audit is complementary to an internal audit, since an external audit carried out by persons from outside the organization guarantees the existence of a higher level of control in the organization.

In view of the above, it should also be borne in mind that the existing relational links between external and internal audits are constantly changing and continue to do so. The sources of such links are global megatrends[14] (civilization trends) with high impact, related to Industry 4.0, digitalization, digitization, development of 5G networks, globalization, or electromobility. Therefore, external and internal audits are also undergoing transformation, creating the next generations of audit, which will be discussed in more detail later in the book.

1.3. Evolution of internal audit against the background of audit generation

Evolution is an ambiguous concept. According to Czachorowski (2010), it can mean: any change, a gradual change – which is not abrupt, a change of a fixed direction – which should be associated with finalism,[15] or a change which should be identified with progress, i.e., the transition from simple to more complex forms, marked by superiority and better characteristics.

Speaking about the evolution of internal audit, or more broadly the generation of internal audit (see Figure 1.2), it should be identified primarily with a change of a gradual, not revolutionary nature,[16] which constantly transforms the audit process toward what is newer, more adequate, but also more complex. However, importantly, this change should not be associated with finality (even indirectly), because we would have to adopt the view that the development of audit tends toward some final – undefined – goal or a previously set limit. Meanwhile, auditing is a matter whose development is not subject to any restrictions, and this means that anticipating any goal to which it is ultimately intended is a task that is not merely difficult but is, in practice, impossible. Undoubtedly, time is also required for something to change or transform. Without it, it is difficult for us to judge whether something has changed or not. The passage of time is, for us, a point of reference, thanks to which we can compare things with each other or objectively refer to something. In the case of the evolution that internal audit has experienced over many years (see Figure 1.1), we can say that its content, form, scope of activity, functions, and the role it performs in the area of finance and

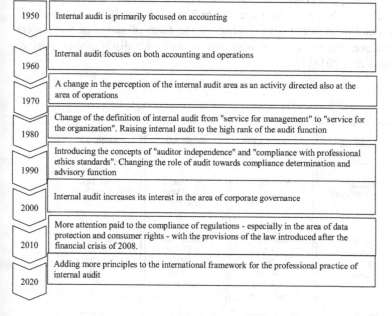

1950	Internal audit is primarily focused on accounting
1960	Internal audit focuses on both accounting and operations
1970	A change in the perception of the internal audit area as an activity directed also at the area of operations
1980	Change of the definition of internal audit from "service for management" to "service for the organization". Raising internal audit to the high rank of the audit function
1990	Introducing the concepts of "auditor independence" and "compliance with professional ethics standards". Changing the role of audit towards compliance determination and advisory function
2000	Internal audit increases its interest in the area of corporate governance
2010	More attention paid to the compliance of regulations - especially in the area of data protection and consumer rights - with the provisions of the law introduced after the financial crisis of 2008.
2020	Adding more principles to the international framework for the professional practice of internal audit

Figure 1.1 Evolution of the role of internal audit – 1950–2020 (in decades) Source: Authors' own study based on RSM International Association, 2019, p. 9, and Buła, 2015a, p. 126.

management of each organization are, over the passage of time, subject to change.

The source of their transformation was primarily the business environment, whose elements in the form of dynamics of economic growth, level of competitiveness, technological challenges, information security, efficiency improvement, aspirations of employees and management, complexity of business activity, legal regulations and procedures, as well as levels and types of risk, have always strongly determined the environment in which internal audit is created and shaped. As a consequence, nowadays it has come to the point that internal audit – especially its role and functions – has been significantly expanded, and at almost all levels of the organization. Today, in times of great political and economic turbulence,[17] it plays a strategic role, providing a continuous overview of business processes and risk areas. Thanks to this, it provides timely valuable information to all stakeholders operating in the organization's environment about the functioning of operational and control mechanisms in it.

The result of the evolution of audit (including internal and external) has been the parallel creation at the global level of its subsequent generations (see Figure 1.2). In practice, these were and still are models of functioning and conducting audit tasks characteristic of a given period or epoch, which, taking into account political, economic, and technological conditions, ultimately determined the form of audit. In the subject literature, the following generations of audit are distinguished (Dai & Vasarhelyi, 2016):

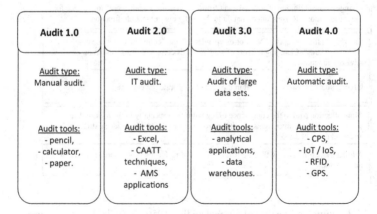

Figure 1.2 Generations of audit – from the past to the present Source: Authors' own study based on Dai and Vasarhelyi, 2016, p. 2.

- Audit 1.0 – the first generation of audit was born with the creation of the IIA in 1941.[18] All audit tasks at that time were performed in a traditional way, i.e., manually. The tools used by the auditors in their work were characterized by extraordinary simplicity and were a pencil, a sheet of paper, a pen, and a calculator (previously an abacus). Audit 1.0 focused its attention more on *ex post* activities than *ex ante,*
- Audit 2.0 – the second generation of audit came with the development of the first era of computerization, which occurred in the 1980s and 1990s, when the first desktop computers became available to ordinary users. Audit 2.0 is referred to as an *IT audit* because IT tools were used for the first time in the form of various types of applications and IT systems, such as Excel, CAATT, or AMS. The CAATT (Computer Assisted Audit Tools and Techniques) system was one of the first IT tools supporting the work of auditors. The same applies to AMS (Audit Management Software), which was a tool used to manage audit tasks. Nowadays, there are more extensive and innovative solutions in the area of these two applications,[19]
- Audit 3.0 – the third generation of audit falls on the first years of the 21st century. Its creation was related to the geometrically growing amount of data and information across the world, which needed to be organized, also in terms of newly emerging risk areas. Hence the idea of the big-data audit, which focused its attention on the review and analysis of selected systems collecting important – from the point of view of the functioning of the organization – data. The new environment in which audit functioned at the beginning of the 21st century also required the use of new tools in the approach to audit tasks, whether in the form of data warehouses or so-called analytical applications (business intelligence systems),
- Audit 4.0 – the fourth generation of audit came at the end of the first decade of the 21st century and should be directly identified with the development of the Fourth Industrial Revolution (Industry 4.0) – a phenomenon that increases the turbulence of the organization's business environment as a result of the permanent development of modern technologies and innovations. The final shape of Audit 4.0 will depend, in a significant way, on the development and innovative technologies promoted by Industry 4.0[20] in the form of cyber-physical systems (CPS), the Internet of Things (IoT), the Internet of Services (IoS), identification of objects using radio waves (Radio-Frequency Identification, RFID), or satellite navigation system (Global Positioning System, GPS). In practice, Audit 4.0 will be a process consisting in the objective collection of information from the Internet, cyber-physical systems, and intelligent (autonomous)

machines and devices that, after analysis and visualization, will identify patterns and deviations from the desired state. Importantly, Audit 4.0 will continue to draw on the experience of Audit 3.0, especially in data analysis and obtaining information necessary for the entire audit task. In light of growing global digitization and digitization of economic life, the skills of auditors will also have to undergo a radical change, who from now on will carry out audit tasks – related to the verification of processes, procedures and transactions – in the environment of intelligent (autonomous) machines, devices, or entire factories.

The audit generations presented above are, in fact, a reflection of the changes that organizations have undergone over the past several decades. Their source was technological progress, which determined the way enterprises function and are managed. The situation is similar today, when innovation and digital transformation[21] are penetrating faster and deeper into various spheres of economic life and all industries, thus posing new challenges to organizations. Consequently, there are changes in the methods of production, in supply chain management, in the organizational structures of enterprises, in the work environment, in interpersonal communication, in data management, or in business models. Importantly, the way of perceiving and managing risk, which is an inseparable element of running any business, is also changing. These changes and challenges require an appropriate audit response, since such a response also needs to be transformed to meet the tasks for which it was formed. What is more, it must be prepared to reliably assess the processes, procedures, or transactions that will be carried out in the new, digital reality. However, this situation may give rise to the risk of audit inaction. Therefore, it must also actively respond to changes taking place in the organization, so that it can continue to play a preventive role in relation to the new risks to which it will be exposed. The transformational changes taking place at various levels of the organization, as well as in its various cells or departments, will also require greater commitment both on the part of the entire management and of the employees. In the case of people responsible for managing the organization, it is not only about using new technologies in audit work, but also about developing a new model that will consider and use the possibilities offered by digital technology, e.g., in the area of analysis of large data sets. In other words, it is about defining a new generation audit that will take into account aspects related to innovation (e.g., the use of artificial intelligence in audit),[22] efficiency, effectiveness of using large data resources, and improvement of risk management.

1.4. Internal audit and controlling – a comparative analysis

Based on management and finance sciences, the issue regarding the occurrence of differences and similarities in relation to internal audit and controlling[23] has been subject to many interpretations and definitions. In practice – paradoxically – this led to a blurring of the essence of both issues, which meant that internal audit and controlling were often treated as synonyms. In addition, it is also not difficult to identify in subject literature the cases in which both these conceptual categories are used interchangeably. Meanwhile, internal audit is not controlling, just as controlling is not internal audit, even though both terms have certain features that are common to each. This section will attempt, for the sake of terminological order, to sort out the essence, differences, and similarities between internal audit and controlling. However, more emphasis will be placed on the issue of controlling, as the concept of internal audit has already been described in more detail in Sections 1.2 and 1.3. However, it should start with the fact that in recent years controlling has become an important tool for influencing the processes taking place in the organization and one of the main instruments shaping the correct "attitudes" in its daily functioning. This is mainly due to the development of the organizational environment, as well as the increase in the popularity of scientific concepts aimed at the continuous improvement and efficient functioning of the institution. In practice, the increased importance of controlling has been reflected in the richness of terms and concepts describing what controlling is, how it should be interpreted in a broad or narrow sense, or what forms it can take based on governing and managing an organization. Controlling is most often defined in management literature as a process thanks to which the management strives to acquire and use the limited resources of the organization as effectively as possible in order to implement the adopted strategy of action. In addition, the frequently cited definitions of controlling also indicate that it is one of the four basic management functions, along with planning, organizing, and motivating. From this perspective, it can be concluded – and rightly so – that controlling, and, in fact, its result, is also the basic determinant of success in the functioning of any organization. Finally, controlling should – as should several of the management functions – be carried out at all levels of the organization in a permanent or periodic manner, so that the management staff can be sure that the tasks performed within the adopted strategy ultimately serve its implementation. The most common definitions of controlling in the literature are presented in Table 1.4.

A careful reading of scientific studies in the field of management in general, and controlling and internal audit in particular, allows us to see that the term "controlling"[24] can be used both in a narrow and a broad sense.

Table 1.4 Definitions of controlling – a literature review

Definitions of controlling	Author/Source
Controlling is one of the management functions performed by managers at all levels of the organization. They are responsible for the tasks assigned to be performed, and at the same time they exercise regular control over subordinates so that the set goals can be achieved	Cambalikova and Misun, 2017
The essence of controlling is not to "assess" whether the planned goals have been achieved but to monitor the progress in achieving the goals	Sljivic et al., 2015
Controlling at the micro- and macroeconomic levels is an essential management function	Ionescu, 2010
Controlling means a comparison between the planned and actual activity, together with the identification of possible corrective actions	Herath, 2007
Controlling is the process of directing a set of variables in order to achieve the assumed result. It's a broad term applicable to people, things, situations, and organizations. In organizations, controlling includes various planning and supervision processes	Anthony et al., 1989
Controlling, as a word referring to the function of management, is about influencing human behavior, because it is people who make something happen in the organization. In other words, controlling is when managers take steps to ensure that people are doing the best for the organization	Merchant, 1985
Controlling processes help to reduce idiosyncratic behavior and maintain its compliance with the rational plan of the organization	Tannenbaum, 1962

Source: Authors' own study.

In a narrow sense, Krzyżanowski (1994) defines controlling as a set of specific activities that consist of examining actual states with tasks, finding deviations, and formulating recommendations, without including them in the scope of corrective and regulatory procedures that belong to the preceding functions. Such an approach to controlling, as Bielińska-Dusza (2011) rightly points out, is strictly reporting and advisory. This means that this type of controlling focuses primarily on establishing the factual situation, which takes place by measuring a given phenomenon in relation to designated paradigms or norms, and then focuses on formulating recommendations to correct the aberrations created in the organization. As part of the narrow approach to controlling,[25] Lisiński (2011) distinguishes the following forms: inventory (so-called physical inventory), overview (preliminary inspection), visitation (direct controlling), safeguarding (direct controlling of the "object"), surveillance (discreet controlling of the "object"), checking (verification), inspection (state control, departmental control, etc.), audit (supplementing current controlling), internal audit, insight (view of the phenomenon), review (check), monitoring (observation and measurement of the phenomenon), internal controlling (process), internal control system (activities, tasks). In broad terms, however, controlling is defined as an activity whose purpose is only to check whether the execution agrees with the plan, i.e., the previously adopted pattern (Adamiecki, 1985). With regard to the organization and its management, it boils down to the systematic supervision of its main representatives over the implementation of the proper course of previously planned activities within the defined strategy.

The broad approach to control differs from its narrow approach in that the authorities supervising or managing a given institution can directly influence its nature and scope, but at the same time they bear greater responsibility for their actions and/or omissions. As part of this approach to control, the following forms are distinguished (Lisiński, 2011): supervision (including the so-called corporate supervision), controlling,[26] self-assessment, and compliance.[27]

Having a basic understanding of the essence of internal audit (see Section 1.2) and controlling, we can see that although they are close and related concepts, they are characterized by a certain distinctiveness. Nevertheless, on the basis of both theory and practice, it is not uncommon to encounter the thesis that audit and control are two completely different activities. As proof of its support, an image is presented (see Figure 1.3) of the controller and the auditor, standing back-to-back, where one looks to the past and the other to the future. Looking into the past is the person of the controller, and into the future, the auditor. Meanwhile – apart from the suggestions contained in the figure – one cannot evaluate audit and controlling in terms

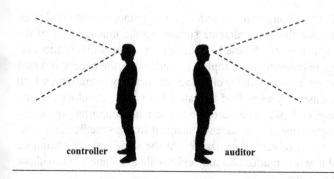

controller   auditor

Figure 1.3 Audit *vs.* controlling – graphic approach Source: Authors' own study.

of black-and-white thinking. These are two conceptual terms which, despite their distinctiveness, have common features and areas that are characteristic of them and which are subject to mutual interpenetration. As an example, it is worth mentioning that both internal audit and controlling are instruments used by management to control risk in the organization or to protect the company's assets against the undesirable actions of its employees or third parties.

In the context of the above, it should be noted that internal audit and controlling are related but still separate terms. There are more differences between them than similarities (see Table 1.5). As an exemplification, it should be emphasized that the starting points for activities in internal audit are the potential risks that are an inherent feature of the organization's functioning in any environment (especially turbulent), while controlling activities are triggered as a result of the existence of irregularities or fraud. Besides, internal audit is a process-oriented activity, not a people-oriented one. Thus, unlike inspections, it seeks to detect inconsistencies inherent in the processes or procedures of the organization and does not focus on detecting and punishing employees guilty of negligence. Consequently, the psychological reaction of employees to the audit and control should also be different – at least in theory. While the auditee will rather hide inconvenient work-related facts, the person who is the subject of audit activities will be inclined to cooperate with the auditor, which should result in providing them with comprehensive information about the functioning of the organization. In addition, audit tasks – implemented constantly and systematically – are carried out through interviews with employees and research and analysis of both documents and systems, while controlling activities – undertaken at random – are carried out using instruments in the form of visitation, revision, inspection, or monitoring. A detailed account of the differences between internal audit and controlling is provided in Table 1.5.

At the end of this section, it is worth mentioning that both internal audit and controlling are those instruments supporting the management of the organization, which should be used in a thoughtful manner that is adequate to the situation. In particular, this applies to controlling, the excess of which may have a negative impact on the efficiency of company operations, which in an extreme case may even lead to a slowdown in its development and even, ultimately, collapse. Therefore, the instruments supporting organization management must be permanently adapted to the specifics and individual requirements of each organization. At the same time, it should be borne in mind that an organization may exist without an audit, but without controlling, it may not.

Table 1.5 Internal audit and controlling – differences

Internal audit	Controlling
The starting point for activities in the area of internal audit arc potential and critical risks resulting from the functioning of a given organization	The starting point for controlling activities in the organization are suspicions related to the existence of irregularities
Independent activity, performed by choice	Activity limited by the scope of the permit, performed on commission
It can be *ex ante* or *ex post*	It can only be *ex post*
It provides the management of a given organization with objective information on how it functions in terms of legality, economics, expediency, reliability, transparency, and openness	Provides the management of a given organization with information on the established facts using control criteria
Verification activity	Checking activity
Focused on improvement	Aimed at searching for irregularities
Strives to confirm compliance	It seeks to confirm non-compliance
Oriented to processes, procedures, etc.	People-oriented (personal responsibility)
No sanctions	Sanctions (penalties)
Providing an advisory function	Preventive function
Supports management	It protects the organization against losses
Supports risk management	Reduces and eliminates risk
Carried out constantly and systematically	Carried out at random
Implemented through conversations with employees, document research, analysis of systems and processes	Carried out through visits, revisions, inspections, monitoring
Planned	Unplanned (element of surprise)
An organization can exist without an audit	An organization cannot exist without control
It is carried out by an internal auditor	It is carried out by a controller
The internal auditor often reports directly to the head of the unit, who ensures that the auditor has both organizational and procedural separation in the performance of their audit tasks	The inspection is carried out by an employee of the control unit or, on the basis of a personal authorization, by an employee delegated to this task by the management of the unit
Internal audit practices performed on the basis of international standards	Performed on the basis of internal procedures
Low costs of realization	It does not generate higher costs
Audit report	Report of the inspection carried out

Source: Authors' own study based on secondary research and Buła, 2015a, pp. 141–2.

1.5. Internal auditor – role, tasks, standards, work

The IIA agrees that the main goal of internal audit, as an independent and objective activity, is to increase the value, and improve the functioning, of the organization. In other words, it is simply about improving a thing and/or processes. This task is carried out primarily through:

- verifying specific items (existing data) and comparing them with established requirements,
- identifying and learning about exceptions,
- review of non-standard things and phenomena,
- reconstruction or correction of identified errors,
- proposing improvements to eliminate exceptions (deviations) in the future,
- assistance in streamlining and stabilizing processes.

The effectiveness and efficiency of the above-mentioned activities that fall within the scope of audit work will depend on the specialist who will carry them out. It is the internal auditor, who is referred to here, that will be responsible for the quality and operability of the audit. To achieve it, an internal auditor must have the right range of skills, knowledge, and knowledge of selected scientific disciplines (e.g., law, management, finance, economics, IT) and be ready to constantly improve their own qualifications, which are somehow connected with the exercise of this profession. In practice, internal auditors are highly trusted researchers, analysts, or advisors who focus on identifying and solving problems that trouble organizations in their daily work. Importantly, they bring to these organizations important values related to matter-of-factness, skills, knowledge, and experience, which constitute a permanent foundation for all internal activities of any company or institution. Nowadays, people who professionally and on a daily basis deal with internal audit, must have, in addition to hard competences (specialist knowledge, knowledge of computer programs and systems, etc.) – as already mentioned – soft competences, i.e., those closely related to the human psyche. This means that the internal auditor must also be able to cope with stress, effectively manage his person, give the ability to self-motivation, and be able to show assertiveness and creativity. In addition, the auditor should have extensive communication skills, such as motivating others to work, delegating tasks, the ability to build and work in a team, or self-presentation skills, so that the auditor can effectively use them in relation with other people, especially during the implementation of audit activities. Soft skills, which allow their owner to behave effectively in certain situations, are nowadays – and not only in relation to the internal auditor profession – of great importance in recruitment processes.[28] Although skills, competences, standards (including standards of professional ethics), and the role played by internal auditors in organizations have already been described in detail and exhaustively in many scientific publications and trade journals, it is still not uncommon for internal auditors to be confused particularly with external auditors but also with accountants and chartered accountants. Meanwhile, the areas of professional interest of both an internal auditor, an external auditor, or an accountant differ – and significantly – from each other, as well as the skills that are needed to perform these professions. The differences between the professions of internal and external auditor are more clearly highlighted in Table 1.6.

In order to supplement the information contained in Table 1.6, it is necessary to recall here 11 basic tasks that have been specified by the IIA and which are carried out by internal auditors in their daily work. They concern (The Institute of Internal Auditors, 2016):

Table 1.6 Internal auditor *vs.* external auditor – scope of activities and competences

Internal auditor	External auditor
Usually employed by the organization in which they work (unless this function is outsourced or as part of periodic cooperation), but the work performed is independent of the area audited	Hired by the organization from the outside, to perform a specific service for it
Wide range of activities:	**Detailed scope of action:**
• risk management • corporate governance • operational and strategic objectives of the organization • operational efficiency and effectiveness • compliance • accuracy of financial statements • process management • other	• correctness of financial statements
Experience and skills:	**Detailed experience and skills:**
• communication skills • interpersonal skills • IT skills • analytical skills (exploration of data) • industry and specialist knowledge• knowledge in the field of accounting	• in bookkeeping and accounting • in auditing accounting books
Ex post and *ex ante* approach	**Mainly *ex post* approach**

Source: Based on The Institute of Internal Auditors, 2016, p. 4, and Buła, 2015a, p. 136.

1) consulting on and verification of projects – the knowledge of internal auditors regarding the mechanisms of the functioning of controlling systems and a holistic view of the organization make them ideal candidates to be project consultants. Thanks to the ability to assess risk, they can take on the role of an advisor who will help solve existing problems. Nevertheless, it is the management that must ultimately take responsibility for the implementation of projects in their areas,

2) risk assessment – due to the fact that the risk is nearly ubiquitous (natural disasters, terrorist and cyberattacks, loss of key suppliers, loss of reputation, fraud, financial embezzlement, lawsuits, violation of legal, moral, and ethical principles), the task of the internal auditor is to identify and assess risk from the point of view of its impact on the functioning of the organization. The auditor should effectively control the risk by transferring knowledge about it to the management of the organization and developing recommendations aimed at its effective management,

3) assessment of controlling (system) – internal auditors assess the efficiency and effectiveness of the functioning of control mechanisms in the organization and issue recommendations to the management as to the correctness of its operation,

4) ensuring accuracy and correctness in the preparation of statements and reports – internal auditors guarantee the reliability and correctness of financial and non-financial statements prepared in the organization. Ensuring accuracy in the reports prepared by the auditors, is made possible by testing the reliability of the information contained in the documents with the facts.

5) process improvement – having knowledge about the organization and its strategic goals, internal auditors analyze the processes and operations taking place in the organization to determine the degree of the efficiency and productivity of the strategic goals,

6) promoting ethical attitudes – professionalism in the internal auditor profession consists in compliance with the principles enshrined in the code of ethics, which guards honesty, reliability, objectivity, and confidentiality in the performance of tasks and audit activities. Thus, detected irregularities should always be subject to appropriate behavior and be reported to the relevant persons, bodies, or institutions,

7) review of processes and procedures – internal auditors examine the correctness of the designed processes and created procedures that are to serve the implementation of both operational and strategic goals of the organization,

8) compliance monitoring – internal auditors assess the degree of compliance of an organization with applicable laws, regulations, contracts, and laws to ensure that senior management meets these requirements. In addition, they monitor the impact of non-compliance on the activities

of the organization and provide information on this subject to the top management,

9) ensuring security – tangible resources (assets), human resources, and intellectual capital (trademarks, patents, etc.) are valuable to any organization and should therefore be subject to special protection and security. Damage caused in this field can, in an extreme case, even lead to the collapse of the organization. Therefore, internal auditors assess the organization's internal procedures to properly protect its assets against theft, fire, or activities inconsistent with applicable law. In addition, they reveal deficiencies in the security systems and recommend better protection of goods,

10) investigating cases of embezzlement and fraud – since fraud (including theft, embezzlement, extortion) can happen in any organization and at any level of it, it is important that the management board grants appropriate powers and powers of attorney to the internal auditor to carry out the so-called audits of detecting economic fraud and investigating possible fraud throughout the organization,

11) communicating work results – after conducting audit activities in a specific area, the internal auditor reports his findings and recommendations to the appropriate organizational unit responsible for their ongoing coordination and supervision.

The scale at which internal auditors carry out the tasks, described above, in the organization depends on several factors, including:

- type of organizational structure (the degree of its management span or the number of management levels),
- stage of development (in the organizational life cycle) at which the organization is located (whether it is the stage of birth, maturity, or maybe aging),
- size of the organization (e.g., micro-enterprise, corporation, holding),
- sector or industry (the organization may operate in the so-called sensitive industry, i.e., fuel, aviation, energy, or gambling),
- legal form of the organization (the legal form of the organization determines the regulations to which it is subject),
- country of origin (national, treaty, international regulations).

With this in mind, we can therefore see that internal auditors have work to do that is not only important and demanding but also covers a wide range of activities to be performed. Consequently, this situation determines the need for internal auditors to have the appropriate knowledge and skills, which is a *sine qua non* condition for the exercise of this profession. According to Sawyer et al. (2003) an internal auditor should have the following qualifications:

- first, the internal auditor should have a thorough knowledge of the standards, procedures, and techniques of internal audit that are necessary for them to perform their work properly. Proficiency is understood here as the ability to properly apply knowledge in situations that may arise and deal with them without the need to constantly refer to research, tests or the help of other people,
- second, the internal auditor should be required to have a very good knowledge of accounting principles and standards, given that they are a person who works intensively with financial documentation and reports,
- third, the internal auditor must have knowledge of the basic principles and functions of management to be able to identify and assess the significance of deviations from good business practices and customs. In fact, it boils down to a situation in which the internal auditor is able to recognize significant deviations (inconsistencies) and, having qualifications, can carry out the research necessary to find the correct solution to the problem,
- fourth, the internal auditor is required to know (a fact signaled earlier) the fundamentals of subjects such as accounting, economics, commercial law, tax law, finance, management, quantitative methods, or IT. Thanks to this, the auditor will be able to quickly identify extensive or potential problems and define their further course in the context of his research,
- fifth, the internal auditor should be skilled in effective forms of communication with others. This will allow the maintenance of proper relationships with customers or other business partners. Proficiency in verbal and written communication will ensure that they will be able to clearly, and effectively, articulate their cases, tasks, assessments, conclusions, or recommendations,
- sixth, persons supervising the work of internal auditors should clearly define the criteria – including the level of education and experience – necessary to occupy positions related to internal audit. In addition, each audit-related position should have the scope of responsibilities and work that have been assigned to it in the context of performing audit activities,
- seventh, in order to meet the requirements of a modern internal audit, people related to it should have certain character traits related to understanding, determination, adaptation, or assertiveness.

The internal auditor profession, which in fact consists of the permanent improvement of existing processes and procedures within the organization, is not only burdensome but also demanding, in terms of better ideas, results, and audit experience. As a result, it is recommended that it be performed in team form, with close cooperation between employees of the entire organization.

1.6. Control and analytical questions

Control questions

1. Explain the etymology of the word "audit" and define its essence.
2. Taking into account the criterion of the subject and the subject of the audit, list its types accordingly.
3. Name the three main categories of audit.
4. Discuss the two main and two auxiliary audit objectives.
5. According to the definition proposed by the Institute of Internal Auditors, internal audit is …?
6. Name the five main differences between internal and external audit.
7. Briefly discuss the essence of the audit generations, from 1.0 to 4.0.
8. Give a definition of the word "controlling."
9. Give a definition of the word "controlling" in narrow and broad terms.
10. Name the five differences between internal audit and control.
11. List five tasks specified by the Institute of Internal Auditors that are carried out by internal auditors in their daily work.
12. Define the scope of activities and competences of the internal and external auditor.
13. Discuss what is the task of an internal auditor related to ensuring the security of the organization.
14. List three factors determining the scale and scope of audit tasks.
15. Discuss the most important qualifications that Sawyer et al. (2003) think an internal auditor should possess.

Analytical questions

1. If we assume that a mission has a clearly defined, long-term goal that an organization strives for, then what is the mission in the case of an audit?
2. The evolution of internal audit is commonly equated with a change of an evolutionary rather than a revolutionary nature. Demonstrate the validity of this statement by discussing the stages and generations of internal audit development from 1950 to the present day.
3. Give examples that would confirm the thesis that "internal audit is not controlling, just as controlling is not, in fact, an internal audit."

4. In your opinion, is the work as an internal auditor burdensome and is it impossible to perform it without appropriate qualifications? What soft and hard skills should a person who does this type of work have?
5. Discuss the trends and new technologies related to the (internal) audit of the future.

Notes

1 The Great Depression is the largest economic collapse in the history of capitalism, which took place in the United States between 1929 and 1933. It was triggered by a sharp decline on 24 October 1929 (Black Thursday) when the prices of all shares on the New York Stock Exchange (NYSE) collapsed, which led to bankruptcies and massive debts chiefly among the American public.
2 ACCA is the largest international organization in the world, associating specialists in the field of finance, accounting, and bookkeeping. For more information, see www.accaglobal.com.
3 It is a set of interrelated activities (activities or tasks), the implementation of which is a condition *sine qua non* to obtaining a predefined result. Each process, with its beginning and end, is in fact aimed at satisfying the needs of customers, both external and external and internal.
4 Competitive advantage is the achievement by the organization of a superior position over its market competition. An enterprise can achieve a competitive advantage in three main areas: quality, price, information.
5 Article 64(1) of the Polish Accounting Act of 29 September 1994.
6 For more on this subject, see: Kuc B. (2002). *Internal Audit, Theory and Practice*. Wydawnictwo Menedżerskie PTM, Warsaw, 2020, pp. 75–80.
7 Founded in 1919, in the United Kingdom (London), it is the leading and the largest organization in the world, associating specialists in the field of management accounting. Currently, it has more than 232,000 members and is present in 177 countries. For more information on CIMA see: www.cimaglobal.com.
8 A person conducting an audit, having qualifications and skills in this area, often regulated by law.
9 Larcker is a professor of accounting and law at Stanford University (California) in the United States. His research focuses on issues related to corporate governance, accounting management, and compensation agreements in organizations.
10 However, it should be made clear that the enterprise's shareholders are always its stakeholders, while the stakeholders are not always its shareholders.
11 Internal audit has become particularly popular as a result of reforms that have been carried out in the United States since the collapses and financial scandals associated with major corporations such as Enron and WorldCom.
12 The IIA is the oldest and largest auditing organization in the world, founded in 1941, in the United States (New York), bringing together internal auditors. Currently, it has nearly 200,000 members around the world. For more information on the IIA, see www.theiia.org.
13 According to Sawyer, internal audit is a holistic and independent assessment of activities carried out by internal auditors that relates to specific operations and tasks in the organization, mainly in relation to authenticity of financial and

operational information, identification and minimization of risks, the efficiency and effectiveness of the use of available resources, or compliance with procedures, policies, and regulations within a given enterprise (both in terms of the internal and external environments of the organization).

14 The precursor of this conceptual category is considered to be American futurologist John Naisbitt, author of the best-selling book *Megatrends: Ten New Directions Transforming Our Lives*, which sold more than 9 million copies in 60 countries around the world.

15 Synthetically, it is the view that everything is moving toward some ultimate goal.

16 From the point of view of audit development, changes considered as revolutionary are those caused by global financial crises, that cause changes in the laws regarding finance, corporate governance, compliance, accounting, accounting, consumer rights protection, privacy, ownership, etc.

17 Such as those related to the outbreak, in early February 2020, of the global COVID-19 pandemic.

18 See endnote 12.

19 For more on this topic, see Szadkowski, B. (2014). Audit support software. *Financial monthly BANK*, July–August, Warsaw.

20 The term "Industry 4.0" first appeared in the public space in 2011, thanks to the industrial fair held in Germany (in Hanover). Use of the term (German original *Industrie 4.0*) was related to the concept of German businessmen, politicians, and scientists who advocated strengthening the competitiveness of German industry in the face of increasing competition from China. Nowadays, in the literature on the subject, we also meet with other forms of the term "Industry 4.0," which should be treated as synonyms, namely: Era of Systems Cyber-Physical (Cyber-Physical System Era, CPSs Era), Industry of the Future, Production of the Future, or 4IR (Fourth Industrial Revolution).

21 Digital transformation is a process that involves transforming business models, optimizing processes implemented in a given organization, building a digital work environment, and changing the current vision of the company. The primary goal of digital transformation is to increase efficiency and reduce risk. For more on this topic, see Ziyadin, S., Suieubayeva, S., and Utegenova, A. (2020). *Digital Transformation in Business*, DOI: 10.1007/978-3-030-27015-5_49.

22 For more on this subject, see American Accounting Association. (2016). Research ideas for artificial intelligence in auditing: the formalization of audit and workforce supplementation, *Journal of Emerging Technologies in Accounting, 13*(2): 1–20, DOI: 10.2308/jeta-10511 and Moffitt, K.C., Rozario, A.M., and Vasarhelyi M. A. (2018). Robotic process automation for auditing, *Journal of Emerging Technologies in Accounting, 15*(1): 1–10, DOI: 10.2308/jeta-10589.

23 Control is a word derived from the French language, from the word *contrerole*, meaning checking, verification, or evaluation.

24 When discussing – in the context of internal audit – the term *controlling*, it is impossible not to mention The Committee of Sponsorship Organizations of the Treadway Commission (COSO), a joint initiative of five private organizations, including the American Accounting Association (AAA), American Institute of Certified Public Accountants (AICP), Financial Executives International (FEI), Institute of Management Accountants (IMA), and the Institute of Internal Auditors (IIA). COSO aims to provide informed leadership in organizations by developing frameworks and guidance on internal control, risk management, and

fraud prevention in enterprises. For more information, see https://www.coso .org/.

25 Cichy (2019) believes that controlling in narrow terms is: comparison plus drawing conclusions from this comparison. For more on this topic, see Cichy, L. (2019). *Management Internal Control in a Public Company in Terms of Comparative Law*. Legal Monographs. C.H. Beck Publishing House, Warsaw.

26 Controlling, in management sciences, is often defined as a new management function. Controlling focuses on the coordination of basic processes taking place in the organization in order to implement the designated operational and strategic tasks.

27 Compliance, in management sciences, is often referred to as compliance management. In practice, it is an activity (tasks) consisting in ensuring the operational activities of the organization with the requirements of national and international law, regulations, procedures, standards, as well as ethical principles applicable in a given sector or industry.

28 For more on this subject, see Ernst & Young (2012). Competences and qualifications sought by employers among university graduates entering the labor market. Results of a survey conducted by the Warsaw School of Economics, the American Chamber of Commerce in Poland and Ernst & Young. Warsaw.

2 Logistics audit

A classical approach

2.1. The enterprise logistics system – definitions, types, treatments

It is an important thesis that, to carry out logistics audit activities, it is necessary to have good knowledge of the logistics system existing within a given economic system (organization, sector, or industry), because it is this very logistics system – including the elements that make it up – that is the subject of verification and evaluation through audit. This chapter is devoted to basic issues related to the existence, scheme, and functioning of the logistics system. However, considerations on this subject should begin with the definition of the very concept of "system." At this point, it should be emphasized mainly that the term "system" is often abused and freely interpreted, especially in the area of broadly understood logistics. This is due to the fact that this concept is defined too widely, which, most likely, has roots in ignorance of systems theory.[1] However, setting aside such divagations, we can conventionally accept after Mynarski (1979), that a system is a set of elements and relationships (dependencies connecting individual elements into a whole) occurring both between these elements and their properties (features of individual elements).[2] In the context of the subject matter, however, the definition of the system proposed in 2005 by the European Logistics Organization (ELO)[3] is more useful – the system is the place in which processes of movement of goods and/or persons occur, where this action is aimed at profit (as is the case in production and commercial enterprises). In this case we are dealing with the so-called economic system, while where the action is not focused on generating profit, as is the case of public institutions, we are dealing with a system of non-profit institutions.

With a general understanding of what a system is, we can now move on to trying to define what a logistics system is. Malindžák et al. (2015) consider that the logistics system (cf. Figure 2.1) is a system that manages, ensures, and implements the flow of materials, information, and financial

DOI: 10.4324/9781003380184-3

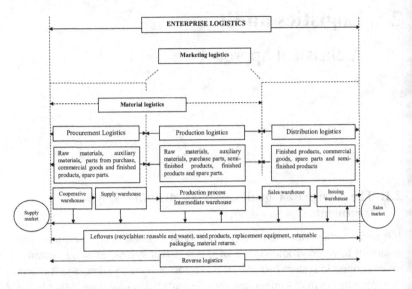

Figure 2.1 The logistics system of the organization in a functional cross-section – graphic approach Source: (Mroczko, 2016, p. 136)

resources. However, they quickly add that, in order to properly define its levels – as a hierarchical system – then, from the point of view of systems theory, it is necessary to first determine the position of the observer (i.e., whether it is a person looking at the organization from within or from the outside). Blaik (2001) presents a similarly broad view of the logistics system presents, considering it to be a set of logistical elements whose connections are formalized and fixed through the processes of transformation taking place. At the same time, he emphasizes that between these elements – with specific features – there occur close and detailed connections (in the organizational sense). A certain complement to the definitions of logistics systems quoted above is the one proposed by Słowiński (2008), who believes that the logistics system is deliberately organized and integrated in the flow of materials and products, and besides, it is an open system because logistics in every aspect is combined with the market and the customer. What all the definitions of a logistics system have in common is that the authors often emphasize the fact that it is not only a connected and integrated system but also consists of many elements, which in practice are reflected mainly in subsystems, including procurement, production, storage, transport, distribution, disposal, planning, steering/guiding, organization, or control. On the other hand, processes take place between the characteristics of individual subsystems that determine the flow of financial resources and information.

When undertaking to characterize a logistics system from the point of view of definitions existing in the literature, one should also know that we can look at a logistics system from both the technical and the functional side (Malindžák et al., 2015). In technical terms, the elements of this system are tools and devices that ensure movement (the flow of people/goods in time and place) including cars, aircraft, ships, railway, conveyors, storage equipment, production lines, robots, transport platforms, cranes, forklifts, transport signaling (e.g., bells).

In the case of material flow, these will be terminals, computers, IT networks, modems, satellites, digital and transmission devices. Speaking about the flow of information, we are dealing with material, information, and financial flows. As far as the functional approach is concerned, in the logistics system it is reflected in the allocation, location, organization, management, and coordination of the flow of materials, products, information, and financial resources. In practice, these are important activities related to the allocation and spatial planning of the organization, including production machinery and equipment, distribution or sales centers, selection of suppliers of products and services, determination of production capacity, preparation of production plans, development of operational and financial plans, design of warehouse space, etc. According to Malindžák et al. (2015), all these activities are closely related and form a chain related to the flows of various objects that are subject to management and which make up the logistic system of functions. In this way, the logistics system (its elements) is finally created,[4] which, according to Kiperska-Moroń and Krzyżaniak (2009), defines:

- the way in which logistics processes take place,
- a set of techniques for carrying out logistics processes,
- a set of means by which logistics processes are carried out.

Like any system, the logistics system is also characterized by specific properties and features, among which we can distinguish primarily those related to:

- a high degree of consistency – in practice this means that a change made within one subsystem automatically entails changes in the other subsystems. This situation is dictated by the fact that there is a high degree of correlation between the various subsystems and the elements that make up it,
- a high level of flexibility – which is reflected in the response of the logistics system to changes taking place in the organizational environment of the enterprise (both internal and external).

At this point, it should also be added that logistics systems are subject to many divisions in the subject literature. One of the most popular is related to the spatial location of logistics systems, where we distinguish:

- macrologistic systems – these include global economic processes taking place on the scale of a state, international organization, or transnational corporation. The obvious result of the macrologistic system is the logistics infrastructure in the form of communication routes, communication systems or sea, land, and airports,
- micrologistic systems – these refer to the logistics of an enterprise and processes related primarily to supply and supply of materials and raw materials, warehousing and storage of goods, production, services, sale, and distribution of products. Micrologistic systems are the basis for the existence (construction) of macrologistic systems,
- metalogistic systems – these are intermediate systems between macrologistic and micrologistic systems. They cover a large number of enterprises and the processes taking place between them. In other words, metalogistic systems are created by micrologistic systems working together.

A characteristic feature of the logistics systems listed above is that (Barcik & Jakubiec, 2011):

- the processes taking place in them, and related to movement (flow) and storage, overlap each other,
- in each of the systems, two spheres can be distinguished, respectively: the sphere of physical flows and the sphere of regulation.

In conclusion, it should be stated that during our lifetime we deal with a huge number of logistics systems. Understanding the specifics of their functioning, even of one, will allow us to understand all the others, including the more complex ones. In order to – in the theoretical part – make it easier to understand the essence of the functioning of the logistics system, we can use an example related to wine production. One of the supply chains is initiated at the time of opencast mining of quartz sand (glass sand), which is the basic ingredient for the production of glass. In this way, a glass bottle is produced. A second supply chain is initiated at the winery, where the winemaker plants the appropriate grape varieties and then harvests them and produces wine from them. Both chains connect in the bottling plant, where wine is poured into glass bottles, which then go onto storage shelves. The analysis of this simple case allows us to see important links in the integrated supply chain (see Figure 3.7). Each of the stages that make up the production of wine is important for the final result. In other words, by linking different supply chains, the entire system is physically merged. Because supply chains are often larger and more extensive, there will be more logistics systems and they will be more complex. And this means that they will be subject to further classifications. Nowadays, it is impossible to achieve market success without achieving success in supply chain management.[5] At this point, it is important to add that the enterprises, which make up the supply chain, are in fact interconnected through a network of physical flows and flows of information. According to Handfield (2020):

- physical flows include the transformation, movement, and storage of goods and materials. In addition, they are the most visible element of the supply chain, and equally important as the flow of information,
- information flows allow different business partners in the supply chain to coordinate their long-term plans and control the current flow of goods and materials, both up and down the supply chain.

2.2. Logistics audit, as an example of an industry audit

There is no doubt that the environment of the organization, especially over the last decade of the 20th century, has become more turbulent and therefore more difficult to predict. The increase in the intensity of changes is dictated primarily by the megatrends[6] related to the development of Industry 4.0 (see Section 2.5) and the threats posed to the global economy by the COVID-19 pandemic. Consequently, these circumstances strongly affect the processes of production, consumption, and investment that take place in many enterprises, as well as the social interactions that are the basic element of the functioning of people and nations. This makes it more difficult to run businesses effectively, which is often associated with maintaining a relatively high level of competitiveness in relation to other market players. That is why, much more often than even a decade ago, management staff reaches for audit as a tool for improving management systems and organizational processes. In practice, it is a source of knowledge about the state of functioning of a given organizational unit in terms of operations, finance, communication, security, or all activities carried out.

Nevertheless, better results are achieved by an audit that is adapted to the specifics of a given industry, including the essence and nature of the processes taking place in it. Hence the rapid increase in the popularity of the so-called industry audits. Jezierski (2007a) argues that industry audits are a source of important information on the condition and effectiveness of a given internal unit of the enterprise. An additional function of industry audits is to disseminate proper control along with the promotion of good changes and patterns and to maintain an optimal level of costs. What is important, in the opinion of Jezierski (2007a), is that industry audits are also a tool used to assess (often critically) the activities of the management staff and individual decision-making links of the organization. In other words, their main task is to provide information necessary for the continuous improvement of processes and systems related to the functioning of a given area and/or organizational unit within a given enterprise. An example of an industry audit is the logistics audit (a type of audit according to its subject – see Table 2.1). Its growing popularity is also the result of – in addition to the previously mentioned phenomena – the interest of enterprises in logistics and the increasingly frequent separation of logistics processes in organizations, which are not only becoming more complex but also play an increasingly important role in the enterprise operations. Hence, as Dendera-Gruszka et al. (2017) rightly point out, the logistics audit has developed as a tool for supervising and controlling logistics processes. Although "logistics audit" is still a relatively new term, the multiplicity of its definitional approaches in the literature on the subject may be surprising. Thus, according to the definition

Table 2.1 Basic objectives of logistics audit

Objectives of the logistics audit:

- Diagnosis of the state of logistics, the logistics system of the organization
- Identification of weaknesses and the possibility of improving the effectiveness of elements forming the organization's logistics system
- Elimination of errors in order to increase the quality of logistics services offered
- Development and implementation of logistic support conditions that will guarantee the continuous achievement of the highest quality of products and/or services
- Identifying opportunities to improve logistics activities in order to meet the requirements and expectations of customers
- Maintaining high quality and efficiency in the process of managing logistics processes
- Gaining the customer's trust in the quality of services and/or products offered, and the level of services provided, in order to increase the likelihood of maintaining constant cooperation with the client
- Ensuring proper relations with the internal and external environment of the organization
- Verification of risk factors affecting the quality of services provided and the costs of the organization's operation
- Accelerating and increasing flows in the logistics system
- Rationalization of logistics costs
- Improvement of operational activities along with optimization of the use of logistics
- Determination of the contribution and effects related to the cyclical conduct of a logistics audit

Source: Authors' own study based on Dendera-Gruszka et al. 2017, p. 26; Żebrucki, 2012, p. 425.

proposed by Klein (2018), a logistics audit analyzes and optimizes – step by step – the overall performance of the enterprise at various operational levels and increases the efficiency of the processes taking place. In addition, it removes bottlenecks that occur in operational processes through the implementation of restructuring activities. As a consequence, the level of service and the quality of logistics increase and logistics areas can be optimally used. Therefore, according to Klein, a logistics audit is the first step to a sustainable improvement in efficiency of the enterprise's operations. Similarly, although more concisely, the same concept is defined by Wawrzynowicz and Wajszczuk (2012), who state that a logistics audit is a systematic and independent analysis aimed at determining whether the activities regarding the quality of the logistics system and their results are consistent with the assumptions. An even simpler definition is proposed by Klug (2018), for whom a logistics audit is a systematic and independent control that diagnoses the logistics system of suppliers or contractors.[7] Žofková and Drábek (2019) also propose a broad approach to the term of logistics audit, stating that a logistics audit simply is a method of comprehensive and independent diagnosis of the enterprise's logistics system. A common feature that binds all the definitions of logistics audit mentioned above is that this audit refers primarily to the verification and then improvement of the logistics system functioning in a given enterprise. In other words, it can be said that a logistics audit is a tool used to check and analyze the discrepancies that occur in the operation of enterprise logistics systems, seeking differences between the declared and the actual state. At this point, however, it should be noted that a logistics audit is about the functioning of logistics systems of enterprises that are located and conduct their activities on different markets, in different sectors and industries. Thus, the specificity of a logistics audit cannot be identified with the TSL sector (transport – shipping – logistics) alone, or with logistics, but it should be treated much more broadly, going beyond the boundaries of the areas of activity listed here. In practice, a logistics audit is an activity that is aimed at achieving three basic objectives (for more, see Table 2.1):

- comparison of the actual state with the declared state (template) in the context of the functioning of the enterprise's logistics system,
- identification and analysis of deviations and dysfunctions occurring within the logistics system,
- providing recommendations and defining areas for improvement in order to eliminate anomalies.

All the presented objectives, in synthetic terms, can be reduced to an objective examination of existing operational processes and logistics flows, and then – on the basis of the collected information – provide recommendations and guidelines on how the logistics system (including logistics processes)

Table 2.2 Processes and areas subject to logistics audit

Processes subject to logistics audit	Areas subject to logistics audit
Warehousing	<ul><li>Organization of warehouse space</li><li>Monitoring of warehousing process</li><li>Freight flows</li><li>Information flows</li><li>Intra-warehouse transfers</li><li>Warehouse infrastructure</li><li>Warehouse security</li><li>Technologies used</li><li>Security of information systems</li><li>Picking and preparation of orders</li><li>Inventory</li><li>Optimization of storage</li><li>Location of materials, goods, finished products, etc.</li><li>Competences of the staff handling warehouse processes</li><li>Personnel management</li><li>Identification of underlying issues</li><li>Warehouse releases</li><li>Release checks</li><li>Directions of improvement</li></ul>
Transport	<ul><li>Organization of transport</li><li>Correctness of rolling stock selection</li><li>Evaluation of route planning</li><li>Efficiency of the rolling stock used</li><li>The right choice of transport (own/external transport)</li><li>Rolling stock replacement policy</li><li>Directions of improvement</li></ul>
Procurement	<ul><li>Supplier classification analysis</li><li>Verification of supplier rating classification</li><li>Quality of service</li><li>Accuracy of providing offer information</li><li>Level of customer service</li><li>Supplier relations</li><li>Communication between individual links</li><li>Information flow</li><li>Delivery time</li><li>Speed of reaction and action</li><li>Ability to take emergency actions</li><li>Providing full information about the status of the order</li><li>Response and action in the event of a complaint or return</li><li>Verification of compliance of deliveries with the order</li></ul>

(Continued)

Table 2.2 (Continued)

Processes subject to logistics audit	Areas subject to logistics audit
Distribution	<ul><li>Network configuration</li><li>Verification and identification of distribution channels</li><li>Level of integration of distribution channels</li><li>Dependency of supporting processes</li><li>Freight flows</li><li>Distribution organization</li><li>Analysis of network strengths and weaknesses</li><li>Directions of improvement</li></ul>
Inventory management	<ul><li>Inventory structure</li><li>Stock size</li><li>Replenishment process</li><li>Inventory rotation</li><li>Directions of improvement</li></ul>
Order fulfillment	<ul><li>Order fulfillment process</li><li>Order structure</li><li>Customer service</li><li>Customer service evaluation</li><li>Complaint and return process</li><li>Costs of order handling</li><li>Directions of improvement</li></ul>
Production	<ul><li>Structure of the production process</li><li>Verification of production orders</li><li>Quality of manufactured products</li><li>Information flow</li><li>Speed of operation</li><li>Production plan</li><li>Accuracy and employee engagement</li><li>Employee competences</li><li>Quality and detail of technological documentation</li><li>Verification of production downtime</li><li>Control of the use of machinery and equipment</li><li>Freight flows</li><li>Production automation</li><li>Machine park replacement policy</li><li>Post-production control</li><li>Production costs</li><li>Process optimization</li><li>Innovation of production tools</li><li>Operation of machinery and equipment</li><li>Maintenance</li><li>Management of repairs and maintenance of machines and equipment</li><li>Quality of corrective actions</li><li>Production reports</li><li>Directions of improvement</li></ul>

(Continued)

Table 2.2 (Continued)

Processes subject to logistics audit	Areas subject to logistics audit
Supply Chain	• Process optimization • Direction of development of supply-chain activities • Verification of the condition of chain links • Supply-chain configuration • Use of infrastructure • Relationships between links • Communication between individual links • Resource flow • Use of modern technologies • Flexibility of operation • Response time to changes • Security of the information flow system • Verification of chain strengths and weaknesses • Directions of improvement
Packaging and secondary raw materials	• Identification and matching of packaging • Operation of packaging • Classification and management of packaging • Packaging recording • Method of recycling and recovery • Storage conditions • Directions of improvement

Source: (Dendera-Gruszka et al., 2017, p. 29).

or supply chain functions for a specific enterprise. In practice, the number of processes or, more generally, areas that can be subject to a logistic audit, is quite significant and concerns a wide range of activities that are carried out as part of the functioning of a given enterprise. In this context, the performance of activities related to logistics audit, even in the area of warehousing, consumes a notable amount of time, because the number of elements that must be tested is large. Table 2.2 presents in detail both the processes and the areas (including individual components) that are subject to a logistics audit within the enterprise.

Often, after a logistics audit has been carried out, a situation occurs in which a process has to be changed or improved so significantly that it is necessary to implement additional procedures and/or update existing ones. Thanks to this, enterprise managers have a detailed description of the procedure that should be followed when performing repetitive activities that will ultimately contribute to the achievement of the intended goals set within the framework of the enterprise's strategy adopted by the management board. Thus, as will be discussed in more detail, an effective logistics audit requires a high level of knowledge about the concepts, methods, techniques, and tools that will serve to improve the productivity of logistics processes.

(e.g. salary, private health insurance, private pension scheme, company car, etc.), learning opportunities and career development, health and safety at work, flexible working arrangements (e.g. part-time, term-time, job share; flex-time; teleworking), equity and fairness at work, involvement in business decision-making and the external environment (e.g. economic pressures, changes in labour regulations, etc.; Panagiotakopoulos, 2014; Mullins and McLean, 2019).

Small firm owners/managers need to take into account all the above-mentioned factors affecting employee job satisfaction in order to enrich staff motivation, thus leading to low turnover and absenteeism, increased participation in learning activities, as well as improved performance. It is crucial for owners to know that human needs differ among people, as well as change across time (i.e. employee needs change as they move into different stages in their life cycle). This means that the process of employee motivation is a dynamic one and requires from the owner to have constant communication with their employees to become aware and understand their personal needs and expectations at each period. The more attuned the small firm owner/manager is to employee needs, the greater the number of matches that are likely to exist in the 'psychological contract' (i.e. the informal agreement between the employee and the owner that specifies what each side expects to give and receive from the employment relationship).

In the small business context, the following 4 specific non-monetary rewards have appeared to be highly effective in boosting staff performance: (a) *staff training*, (b) *challenging work*, (c) *job autonomy* and (d) *work flexibility*. A relevant research study conducted by the author in 2014 on the main factors affecting staff motivation in small firms during periods of severe financial crisis revealed that employee involvement in decision-making, recognition of contribution, team working and continuous learning were among the key rewarding tools that could boost staff motivation. The findings showed that those owners who adopted an 'inspirational motivation' model (e.g. show empathy to employee needs and design meaningful job tasks for employees) managed to achieve far better organizational results in the long term (e.g. reduced staff turnover, improved productivity) compared to those owners who adopted a 'fear motivation' model (e.g. autocratic leadership with punishment being used as the main tool for performance improvement). The latter faced declining staff morale and increased staff occupational stress resulting in increased employee errors and reduced staff loyalty.

As the preceding analysis indicates, employee rewards are a key variable that has a direct impact on the extent of learning in the small business context. If employees realize that they will be rewarded for improving their knowledge base, then they will be much more enthusiastic about engaging in various informal learning activities in order to acquire and apply new skills at work (e.g. moving an employee to a post that involves more interesting and varied tasks after a successful process of skill acquisition could be an important reward for several individuals). An increasing commitment to learning is central when it comes to skills development.

The employment relationship and employee involvement schemes

The steps that small firm owners take to create a harmonious working environment (i.e. healthy and productive relationships with their employees) affect the staff motivation towards skills development. In particular, how owners deal with any employee grievances, the extent of health and safety at work (i.e. employee welfare policies), staff participation in decision-making are just some of the core areas in the field of employee relations that can trigger (or hinder) employee learning.

Regarding grievances, this term is related to the complaints that are presented to the small firm owner/manager by employees. In general terms, grievances are rarely being raised in the small business context since employees do not wish to have a conflict with the firm owner (e.g. by questioning their authority and knowledge), as well as take the risk of being considered as the troublemaker within the enterprise. Additionally, many employees consider this process meaningless since no major change is being implemented as a result of their complaint. However, despite the above arguments, small firm owners/managers should encourage the proper use of communication channels to discover sources of discontent among their staff because the dissatisfaction employees experience from various external or internal factors can lead to poor performance and unsatisfactory work outcomes (e.g. reduced effort, absenteeism, etc.; Panagiotakopoulos, 2016).

Small firm owners can take a number of key steps (as outlined next) towards creating a harmonious working environment that will, in turn, affect the extent of workforce skills development. More specifically, small firm owners/managers need to (a) increase employee participation in decision-making. Employees feel bonded to the organization if they participate in various business decisions and more motivated to participate in various learning interventions. Also, major learning gaps can be identified and discussed; (b) devote much time to employee concerns to understand the obstacles they may face at work (from various factors) and contribute towards performance improvement. The arrangement of frequent social events with employees and the firm owner/manager may be a good opportunity for the sharing of concerns, and (c) be fair and consistent with all employees with any action they take in relation to grievance resolution.

Employee involvement is also a key process that can promote employee learning significantly. The particular process allows employees to develop their knowledge and skills by giving them the opportunity to share their views, ideas and concerns with small firm owners/managers in order to diagnose and solve daily operational problems, as well as address more strategic issues (e.g. ideas on the development of new products/services). Examples of involvement mechanisms include team-working and communities of practice, which were discussed in Chapter 3. Also, the arrangement of formal monthly meetings and the encouragement of daily informal dialogues between owners and employees are also useful practices that can facilitate skills development.

Business example on the interlink of HRD with other HR activities

Case study: 'Leather-T'

The company has been operating for 22 years and manufactures and sells high-quality leather goods (e.g. bags, wallets, belts) to the end users (both wholesale and retail customers) in the U.S. market. The firm is owned by a very experienced entrepreneur (with a business educational background), who has several years of work experience in the specific sector. The organization has 14 employees all of which are full-time, including 10 machine operators who are responsible for the operation and maintenance of the machines, 2 salespeople who deal with all the selling-related activities, 1 general secretary responsible for various administrative tasks (e.g. invoices, fax duties, incoming calls, customer complaints, etc.) and 1 production supervisor, who is responsible for the division of labour, daily flow of production and repairs to machinery. There are no part-time or temporary workers and most of the staff are long-serving. The company sells its products solely in the home market. As for the educational level of personnel, the production supervisor has a business-related degree, whilst the rest of the workers have completed upper-secondary education. The level of technology in the company is fairly modern with all the technological equipment imported from abroad.

The firm owner undertakes all the main responsibilities for employee selection, performance appraisal, training and rewards. Recruitment is carried out mostly through existing employee referrals (networking), whereas selection is based on a formal interview with the owner. The main criteria of staff selection for most posts are previous experience in the particular industry, very good interpersonal skills and willingness to share knowledge, whereas formal education qualifications carry very little weight. Also, there is a formal performance appraisal every 6 months, whilst rewards are based on individual performance (e.g. whether machine operators show initiative or not, as well as problem-solving abilities). Performance appraisal appears to serve as a key tool for skills development within the firm. During the appraisal process, the development needs of the workers are considered, whilst achievement is recognized and reinforced. In terms of employee involvement, at the end of each month there Is a scheduled staff meeting where all employees share their ideas on performance improvement and discuss any work-related issues. The owner welcomes any suggestions on product/service development and provides praise and financial rewards to those employees who will make insightful suggestions that will benefit the organization. For example, a retail voucher is provided to the person whose suggestion will be implemented in the company, whereas there is a generous annual bonus to the person who acted as a mentor to more junior employees.

In terms of workforce skills development, the company does not have a formal training policy and plan. Employee training is implemented according to existing business needs and it is predominantly reactive with no previous planning. The firm owner takes all the decisions around the level and breadth of training provision, and he is also responsible for all the learning activities within the firm. All machine operators undertake on-the-job training on a regular basis around technical issues (e.g. working methods and quality standards) through informal coaching, as well as around various health and safety topics through manuals and formal meetings. Also, there is continuous coaching on the salespeople by the owner in order to improve their interpersonal skills and selling techniques. A large amount of learning also takes place through peer cooperation. In short, teamwork appears to be an effective learning mechanism within the firm. The machine operators work in teams, thus having plenty of opportunities to impart tacit knowledge to each other. Specifically, the more experienced workers act as team leaders for the less experienced machine operators. In this way they act as facilitators to get the most out of production workers and to encourage learning. In terms of their team leadership styles, they appear to be democratic as they listen to team members, question them to understand their points of view and be responsive to feedback.

DISCUSSION

The preceding business case shows how the synergy of various HR activities can contribute significantly towards workforce skills development. As the analysis revealed, the specific organization does not have a formal plan in relation to human resource development and there are no specific financial resources allocated to employee training. Staff development is implemented in a purely informal manner. However, it is fully supported by several other core HR activities including staff selection, performance appraisal and rewards. In particular, the company places much emphasis on a range of 'soft skills' during the employee selection process that seem to benefit knowledge sharing. Moreover, there is a formal performance appraisal mechanism to facilitate skills development along with suitable rewards for knowledge creation. Employee involvement and job design also seem to be critical elements in the process of skills development.

Reflective Case Study

'*PharmU*' is a sales and marketing organization in the U.K. connected to a major global pharmaceutical manufacturing and retailing company that is based in the U.S. (i.e. parent company). It has responsibility for the brand planning and promotion of a number of pharmaceutical products manufactured by the parent company that are very well known in the U.K. It is 1 of 7 business units controlled via the parent company's corporate centre. The corporate centre attempts to bring coherence to the direction in which all the business units are moving. This underpins not only the rationale for strategic decisions taken across all business units but also the way in which individual performance is managed.

PharmU employs 40 people and is structured into 4 core functions (i.e. sales, marketing, finance and human resource management) of which the two largest are sales and marketing. In PharmU, there was no knowledge management strategy in the previous years, but this has changed recently as a result of a visit to the U.S. by the chief executive of the company and the director of finance. Following this, an explicit knowledge management strategy was developed with the aim to break down barriers between teams that inhibited the sharing of knowledge across the organization. In particular, the following major changes were introduced:

- New performance goals were set. All employees were asked to reduce costs and increase profitability, as well as consider how what they do contributes to the 'bottom line' of the business. A strong emphasis on measurable targets was placed.
- There was a decentralization of the recruitment and selection process so that each function in the company could hire suitable people that would fit specifically into their teams (e.g. the marketing function could recruit in their own likeness – blue-suited young women who are prim and proper, whereas the sales function could recruit in their own likeness – brash young men who are very competitive).
- Re-organization of the physical environment so that knowledge sharing could be facilitated among employees of each function. In particular, every function had its own offices all on the same floor.

Tasks

- Do you believe that the course of action taken at PharmU will facilitate knowledge sharing among employees?
- What other measures (if any) would you consider taking? Please justify your suggestions using relevant theory.

Key points of the chapter

The effectiveness of HRD is strongly affected by all the other HR functions, including HR planning, recruitment, selection, performance appraisal, rewards and employee relations. All these core HR activities are heavily interlinked, and their synergy is central to any employee learning intervention.

Accurate labour forecasting can ensure that the organization has the right number of employees when needed. This means that there will be no further requirements for intensive training of existing staff in order to cover any labour shortages. Careful recruitment and selection can ensure that employees have the right type of hard and soft skills in order to perform effectively in their jobs. Regular performance appraisals can lead to the effective diagnosis of employee learning needs and performance gaps. Rewards that promote and encourage knowledge sharing are necessary for employee skills development since they stimulate the process of social learning. Employee involvement is also crucial for workforce skills development since it can inform small firm owners/managers about the exact learning needs of employees and ways to improve their performance.

References

Mullins, L. and J. McLean (2019) *Organisational behaviour in the workplace.* 12th ed. London: Pearson.

Panagiotakopoulos, A. (2014) 'Enhancing staff motivation in tough periods: implications for business leaders', *Strategic Direction*, vol. 30, no. 6, pp. 35–36.

Panagiotakopoulos, A. (2016) *A short guide to people management for HR and line managers.* London: Routledge Publications.

Stone, R. J. (2002) *Human resource management.* 4th ed. Milton: John Wiley and Sons.

5 Leadership and staff learning

Definition, importance and theories of leadership

The importance of leadership for small firm performance and staff learning cannot be over-emphasized. Normally, the owner of the small firm has the role of the leader who communicates the vision of the company to all employees, sets the overall business strategy, guides and trains staff towards achieving the business objectives and manages the change process within the enterprise. Several research efforts have pointed to the various benefits that effective leadership may bring to staff and the company itself, such as improved employee motivation and commitment and increased staff adaptability, as well as enhanced employee learning capacity that may result in an increasing rate of product/service innovation. The leader is also the person that can initiate strategic change, as well as guide their staff on how to manage uncertainty effectively. This is highly important in the turbulent macro-environment where most small firms operate (Anderson, 2010; Panagiotakopoulos, 2014; Buck, 2016).

There is extensive research on the factors affecting leadership effectiveness. A rigorous historical overview reveals that several theoretical models have been put forward in order to explain why some leaders are more successful than others with each theory having its own strengths and limitations (e.g. trait-based theories, behavioural theories, contingency theories, transactional theory, transformational and charismatic theory, collaborative leadership theory). Yet, a central argument of all these theories is that there is no specific leadership approach that can ensure success in every micro/macro-environmental context. The vast array of factors that come into play within an organizational environment require an equally complex set of responses in order to lead effectively a team of employees and stay ahead of the competition (Northouse, 2015).

The theory of *charismatic leadership* can be applied in the small business context and has the potential to achieve some positive organizational outcomes. This theory argues that an effective leader is one who is able to recognize the needs of their employees, communicate in a clear manner

DOI: 10.4324/9781003381815-6

the company's vision, as well as inspire and guide staff in order to achieve the organizational goals. This is essentially achieved through employee commitment. Charismatic leadership depends predominantly on the personality and actions of the leader and not the process or structure. Charismatic leaders have excellent interpersonal skills and a very high level of emotional intelligence. They have also developed some very clear and specific goals, which have been properly articulated to their staff. Moreover, they are those people who will take reasonable risks, which are deemed to be profitable and rewarding for the business (Zehndorfer, 2016). At the heart of charismatic leadership is the leader's ability to adopt a positive stance towards every challenge, as well as being a moral role model for their staff (i.e. the leader's ethical stance is exemplary), as well as inspire and motivate them to have superior performance.

The particular theory has several strengths as a theoretical concept and this is the reason why it is widely applied in many organizations. Compared to the previous theories that recognize the cognitive features of the relationship between leaders and followers, the charismatic leadership model emphasizes the importance of emotional reactions by subordinates to leaders. In simple terms, it highlights what followers need in order to be motivated to contribute to a common goal (Mumford *et al.*, 2000). Furthermore, another strong point of the particular theory is that it can lead to various long-term positive outcomes for the company that may enable the firm to gain a sustainable competitive advantage (not just superior short-term performance).

For example, during the last decades, lots of firm owners in the small business sector across the world used a 'fear motivation' approach (based on the transactional leadership paradigm) in order to boost staff performance. The fear motivation approach is based on the notion that employees will work hard to maximize their performance for fear of losing their jobs in periods of severe economic recession and high unemployment (i.e. in labour markets where the unemployment rate is very high). However, recent empirical evidence in this area has shown that this approach brings very few short-term benefits, whereas in the long-term it leads to detrimental consequences for organizations since employees suffer from burnout and are unable to go the extra mile. Their productivity is seriously reduced, and there is high staff turnover as soon as alternative employment options become available (Panagiotakopoulos, 2014). Therefore, gaining staff commitment through an inspirational leadership approach is the suggested path for small firm owners to ensure superior employee performance. This leadership approach has also some important implications for employee learning. In particular, it can ensure that talents are fully developed and employees fulfil their potential. A charismatic leader is also a competent mentor for their employees, thus contributing towards their personal and professional development.

Although the charismatic leadership model has a lot of positive characteristics, yet it comes with a few conceptual limitations. Despite the fact that it provides a detailed explanation of the influence between the leader and their followers, it does not indicate exactly how this could be operationalized at the workplace. More specifically, this theory is mainly leader-centred, and it emphasizes the influence of the leader on followers. However, it is not sufficient to explain in detail how leaders could build exceptional teams (Yukl, 2006; Avolio and Yammarino, 2013). This publication makes an initial attempt to fill this knowledge gap. Hence, in the next sections, an analysis is being undertaken (using empirical evidence) on how leaders could build high-performing teams.

Emotional intelligence and leadership

One of the core concepts in the area of small firm leadership is emotional intelligence (EI). This is a term used to denote the ability of an individual to understand and manage both their own emotions and those of others (Goleman, 1995). For small firm owners, having a high degree of EI is essential for personal and professional success since it determines the quality of any decision made (including any learning interventions). For example, those small firm owners that have developed their EI can easily identify employees that lack confidence at work and consequently can provide them with proper learning interventions to boost their self-confidence. Emotional intelligence consists of 4 core elements:

Self-Awareness: This is the individual's ability to understand their own emotions. This ability helps people become aware of their strengths and weaknesses. Also, it helps them understand the root of their feelings in order to manage them effectively (e.g. able to manage their stress, anger, distress). There are several practical ways that can help busy firm owners to develop their self-awareness including personal journals where feelings and thoughts can be written down. Then, the next step is to examine *'why'* certain feelings emerged in specific social situations.

Self-Regulation: This is the individual's ability to manage effectively their own emotions and impulses. All the existing research studies have shown that people who are capable of managing their feelings do make well-informed decisions. In the small business context, firm owners are usually under continuous stress since they are heavily involved in all the core business activities. Hence, managing stress effectively is of the utmost importance in order to be able to lead effectively their teams. Research from the field of industrial psychology indicates that the ABCDE technique (originally developed by Albert Ellis in the 1950s) can provide the starting point for the successful management of occupational stress. This cognitive behaviour therapy model essentially involves 5 steps as described very briefly here:

1   A (activating agent): the step where you attempt to identify the stressor.
2   B (belief system): the step where you explore in-depth your existing belief system and you attempt to identify rational and irrational beliefs.
3   C (consequences): the step where you try to identify the mental, physical and behavioural implications of the stressor.
4   D (dispute irrational beliefs): this is the crucial step where you try to challenge your initial beliefs by findings new frames of reference to support your new thoughts. Through extensive self-reflection, you can remove cognitive distortions (e.g. over-simplified generalizations) and reconsider any negative experience as a positive one.
5   E (effects of cognitive restructuring): in this last step you attempt to measure the effects of changing your interpretation of a situation (i.e. you evaluate the outcome of cognitive-behavioural change).

Empathy: This is equally a very important element of emotional intelligence. Empathy is the ability of an individual to identify and understand the needs and viewpoints of those around them. People with empathy are good at recognizing the feelings of others, even when those feelings may not be obvious, and support them towards unleashing their potential. In short, these people manage to build excellent personal and professional relationships. They avoid stereotyping and judging too quickly, as well as they live their lives in a very honest way.

A useful practical process that may help an individual develop their empathy is by trying to look at a situation through the perspective of the other person (i.e. different perceptual lenses). In simple terms, it is important for individuals to develop a sound awareness of why other people feel, think and behave the way they do. For example, small firm owners should consider the general background of each employee (e.g. family, education, social status, cultural values, etc.) in order to understand the underlying reasons for their behaviour. In this context, they will be able to guide them properly and support them towards achieving the business objectives.

Social Skills: This set of skills involves a range of abilities (e.g. listening skills) that help individuals communicate effectively with other people. Excellent interpersonal skills do help people share their ideas and knowledge, manage conflicts and negotiate action. Individuals that have developed their social skills are excellent team players since they are able to listen carefully to others' concerns, as well as help them develop and excel at work. A starting point for owners to hone their social skills is by developing their listening skills. For example, when listening to employee concerns, it is important to remove any distractions that may take place at work, make employees feel relaxed and summarize an explanation given by an employee on a particular issue. Instead of focusing on preparing their immediate response, it is important for owners to place much emphasis on listening to their employees and understanding their needs.

The preceding concise analysis shows that EI is not learned through a traditional learning method (e.g. classroom-based teaching). Essentially, it must be learned in an experiential manner since it requires a rigorous exploration of the emotional sphere. The specific type of learning is based on what we actually see, hear and feel. Daniel's Goleman (1995) work on EI has been very influential in the business arena, so small firm owners should explore extensively this core thematic area for organizational success.

Leadership and informal teams

In the contemporary business arena, most work is rarely undertaken in complete isolation. Employee cooperation (i.e. team working) has become the norm, and almost every individual within an organisation will be a member of one or more groups. This has also significant implications for learning. The more people collaborate the more they learn through the process of social learning. Therefore, it is important to examine how small firm leaders can create high-performing teams and how they can encourage the development of informal teams that may contribute towards skills acquisition.

Starting with a short working definition of a team, it can be argued that a team is a group of 2 or more people who interact with each other (plus there is interdependence), are psychologically aware of one another (i.e. perceive themselves to be a group) and try to achieve a common business goal. Teams can be either *formal* or *informal*. Formal teams are created by small firm owners/managers in order to complete a range of complex work-related tasks and projects, whereas informal teams arise from the personal relationships among employees, irrespective of those defined within the formal organizational structure.

Informal teams may offer various advantages to both employees and firm owners. In particular, they can improve employee job security since they provide workers with a powerful collective voice (e.g. in case of unfair dismissals). Furthermore, they can facilitate significantly the process of skills development through staff collaboration (i.e. social learning). In particular, knowledge sharing among employees can be a vital process towards skills acquisition. However, informal teams have their own limitations and may affect firm performance in a negative manner. For example, informal teams may encourage their members to adopt norms that contradict the prevalent business culture (e.g. lack of punctuality), which may consequently affect the overall organizational performance.

It is vital for small firm owners to understand that informal teams are likely to be developed in organizational contexts where a charismatic leadership model is applied rather than in contexts where the emphasis is placed on legitimate authority and power. Also, informal groups generally meet social and security needs before other needs. Given the previously mentioned benefits of informal teams, it should be among the key roles of small firm owners/managers to facilitate the development of informal teams (e.g. through various social events and activities) but at the same time encourage them to match their aspirations with those of the whole organization. Below are given some guidelines on how small firm owners can support the creation and growth of both formal and informal teams (Panagiotakopoulos, 2016):

- Place much emphasis on the composition of the team since this will affect the rate of learning. Meredith Belbin stressed long ago that teams need to consist of individuals who have certain behavioural traits that enable them to play specific roles. These are the *coordinator* who has a clear view of the team objectives and organizes the team activities, the *shaper* who can get things going, the *plant* who is likely to develop some original ideas, the *resource investigator* who has extensive social contacts and can build networking, the *implementer* who can easily put theory into practice, the *team worker* who tries to promote harmony within the team, the *completer* who sets the deadlines and ensures they are achieved, the *monitor evaluator* who can critically evaluate all the available options for action and the *specialist* who provides specialist skills and knowledge around a particular subject area.
- Set clear, challenging and interdependent tasks so that employees can interact with each other towards their completion. This will stimulate the process of social learning.
- Create a proper physical setting that gives the opportunity to staff for increased social interaction (e.g. shared offices).
- Arrange certain social events during the year to encourage informal team development and bonding.
- Provide team rewards for outstanding performance, as well as for knowledge sharing. Recognizing team excellence through monetary (e.g. bonus) and non-monetary rewards (e.g. verbal praise), for example, can enhance team motivation significantly.

- Hold each member accountable for team performance to minimize the phenomenon of 'social loafing' (i.e. a team member puts less effort than the rest).
- Encourage team autonomy to increase members' satisfaction. Several studies have shown that small firm owners/managers are usually reluctant to grant decision-making authority to their staff for fear of losing their negotiating power at work. However, this limits the ability of employees to expand their knowledge and skills, as well as reduces their job satisfaction. As a result, their motivation is seriously damaged and translated into poor performance with a negative impact on the whole organization.
- Provide proper resources (e.g. tools, budget) to the team in order to achieve the business objectives.
- Provide continuous coaching. Any team project should also be viewed as a valuable learning experience.

Reflective Case Study

'Hotel Z' is a 5-star luxurious hotel chain consisting of 40 hotels throughout the U.K. The organization recently acquired a 5-star hotel in Spain in order to expand further to the European region. The hotels of the parent company are situated in very popular locations and offer high-quality services to customers with a premium on price. The organization has decided to use an ethnocentric approach and send one of its existing high-calibre (U.K.-based) managers to Spain to lead the acquisition process and transfer some core corporate values. If this new international venture is successful, the organization plans to acquire some more hotel groups in other European countries. After a rigorous screening process, the senior leaders of the parent company ended up identifying 2 potential candidates who had the required skills and expressed their willingness and desire to relocate. After a series of in-depth interviews and personality tests, the leaders created a comprehensive profile for each candidate, which follows:

Candidate A:

- Marital status: single
- Age: 45
- Very good knowledge of Spanish
- Excellent analytical skills
- Career-oriented
- High emotional resilience
- 3 years' previous international experience
- 5 years' work experience in Hotel Z

Candidate B:

- Marital status: Married
- Age: 38
- Very good knowledge of Spanish
- Excellent analytical skills
- Career-oriented
- High emotional resilience
- 5 years' previous international experience
- 7 years' work experience in Hotel Z

Candidate's B wife was also interviewed. She does not speak Spanish, but she was very enthusiastic about moving to Spain. She fluently speaks English, German and French and has worked previously as a receptionist for 7 years in a small U.K. hotel. After the final round of interviews, the selection panel chose Candidate A. The selection criteria used follow:

Selection criteria:

- Analytical/problem-solving skills
- Interpersonal skills/conflict management skills
- Stress management skills
- Time-management skills
- Technical skills (IT)
- Extent of extraversion–introversion
- Marital status
- Age
- Previous international experience
- Language skills
- Employment history within the company

Tasks

After ranking (in order of importance) the preceding selection criteria, critically evaluate the selection process and the leaders' final decision on the chosen candidate. Use relevant theory to support your arguments.

Key points of the chapter

Leadership is critical for a small firm's success since the leader is the person who creates the future direction of the organization and inspires followers to support them towards achieving business objectives. Leaders who adopt a participative style tend to promote staff learning and stimulate social learning among employees.

EI is vital for small firm leaders since it can enable them to build high-performing teams that will work towards achieving business objectives and will be able to respond to any unpredicted environmental changes. EI consists of 4 core elements: the ability of an individual to understand their own emotions, the ability to effectively manage their emotions, the ability to understand other people's needs and the ability to manage effectively their social relationships.

The creation and support of both formal and informal teams in the workplace are crucial for the completion of several daily tasks and skills development. Therefore, small firm owners should take a number of steps to create high-performing teams, including careful selection of team members, setting of clear and challenging goals, extensive coaching, feedback provision on team performance and team rewards.

References

Anderson, M. (2010) *The leadership book*. London: Financial Times/Prentice Hall.

Avolio, B. and F. Yammarino (2013) *Transformational and charismatic leadership: the road ahead*. 10th anniversary edition. Bingley: Emerald Publishers.

Buck, A. (2016) *Leadership matters*. Suffolk: John Catt Educational Publishers.

Goleman, D. (1995) *Emotional intelligence*. New York: Bantam Books.

Mumford, M. D., Zaccaro, S. J., Harding, F. D., Jacobs, T. O., and Fleishman, E. A. (2000) 'Leadership skills for a changing world: solving complex social problems', *The Leadership Quarterly*, vol. 11, no. 1, pp. 11–35.

Northouse, P. (2015) *Leadership: theory and practice*. 7th ed. London: Sage Publications.

Panagiotakopoulos, A. (2014) 'Enhancing staff motivation in tough periods: implications for business leaders', *Strategic Direction*, vol. 30, no. 6, pp. 35–36.

Panagiotakopoulos, A. (2016) *A short guide to people management for HR and line managers*. London: Routledge Publications.

Yukl, G. (2006) *Leadership in organizations*. Hoboken: Prentice Hall Publications.

Zehndorfer, E. (2016) *Charismatic leadership*. Oxon: Routledge Publications.

6 International dimensions of employee learning in small firms

Cross-cultural challenges of small organizations and implications for learning

In the current era, a large number of small organizations engage in international business activities in order to gain access to unique raw materials, acquire access to larger markets (thus increasing their potential for profitability) and find cheaper production methods, as well as acquire access to advanced technology and know-how. The intense domestic competition in various sectors has forced small firm owners to turn their attention to the global business arena in order to survive or/and increase profitability. However, as companies cross national borders, the business environment becomes more complex compared to the domestic macro-environment since additional factors come into play (e.g. the political, social, legal, economic environment varies significantly among countries). In this context, a sound knowledge of the impact of culture on employee work attitudes is necessary if small firm owners are to support staff learning and boost organizational performance.

National culture is defined as the set of norms, behaviours, beliefs and customs shared by the population of a sovereign nation. Also refers to specific characteristics such as language, religion, ethnic and racial identity, history and traditions (Hofstede, 1980). Extensive cross-cultural management research has revealed that the national culture shapes human behaviour, so it affects the way people interact and behave at work. Therefore, all business processes that involve human activities are affected by national culture. Several cross-cultural models have attempted to capture the differences in how people behave at work. Hofstede's (1980) cross-cultural theoretical model has been among the most popular ones used in the International HRM literature to demonstrate the cultural differences that exist among employees around the globe and how their impact on staff behaviour.

The Hofstede model of national culture consists of 6 dimensions. The cultural dimensions represent independent preferences for one state of

DOI: 10.4324/9781003381815-7

affairs over another that distinguish countries (rather than individuals) from each other. It should be pointed out that the country scores on the dimensions are relative (i.e. each human being is unique, so culture can only be used meaningfully by comparison). For simplicity of analysis, we will focus on the following 4 core dimensions:

- *Power distance.* This dimension measures the extent to which inequalities in power (social and economic) are accepted within a nation. Countries that have a high score in that dimension are tolerant of wider social and economic inequalities. In the workplace, this means that employees do accept a hierarchy at work and expect to be told what to do (i.e. job autonomy is very limited).
- *Uncertainty avoidance.* This dimension measures the extent to which the members of a society feel uncomfortable with uncertainty and ambiguity. In other words, this dimension tries to capture whether a society is quite tolerant of precarious situations or not. In the workplace, this means that people in countries with a high score in this dimension are usually reluctant to embrace change and prefer stability. Also, they place much emphasis on job security.
- *Individualism versus collectivism.* This dimension measures the extent to which people in a society are integrated into groups. Individualistic societies place much emphasis on caring for self and immediate family members, whereas in collectivist societies, the emphasis is placed on group relations. In the workplace, this means that employees in individualistic societies care mostly about the achievement of personal goals, whereas employees in collectivist societies care mainly about group performance.
- *Masculinity versus femininity.* This dimension attempts to measure the general orientation of a society towards rewards. The masculinity side of this dimension represents a preference in society for achievement, heroism, assertiveness and material rewards for success. Its opposite, femininity, stands for a preference for cooperation, modesty, caring for the weak and quality of life. In the workplace, this means that employees in masculine societies are mostly motivated by financial incentives, whereas employees in feminine societies are predominantly looking for work–life balance.

Using Kolb's experiential learning model (as discussed in Chapter 3) and Hofstede's cultural framework, the impact of national culture on employee learning could be analysed. As mentioned in Chapter 3, people have different learning styles. This means that there are individuals who learn through action and individuals who are abstract thinkers. Furthermore, people from different cultures do have different values and experiences, so for example, their readiness for *classroom-based* learning may be quite different (i.e. learners are receptive to practical or theoretical stimuli depending on their cultural backgrounds). Moreover, as a result of different behaviour patterns, socialization and work experiences, individuals from different cultures may make different assumptions about what they see and understand. Hence, they are likely to acquire different bodies of knowledge. It is therefore important for small firm owners to understand how different cultural backgrounds shape human behaviour towards skills acquisition so that they can design suitable learning interventions.

For example, employees in collective societies such as China, Bangladesh, Portugal and Romania do enjoy peer interaction, so learning through *communities of practice* should be encouraged. By contrast, in individualist societies like the U.K. and U.S., a *classroom-based* approach or/and *self-directed learning* should be used to promote employee skills development. Moreover, employees in countries that score high in power distance expect to receive detailed orders and specific guidance from their superiors on how to complete their tasks. This means that their learning is rather restricted since their senior managers have much control over their informal learning at work compared to low-power-distance countries where employees enjoy greater equality in social status and knowledge sharing can be facilitated and stimulated.

Reflective Case Study

'*LandtechX*' is a very large and profitable information technology (IT) company with its headquarters in the *U.S.* The company manufactures and sells high-quality software payroll systems for small and medium-sized organizations. A year ago, the company acquired a well-known IT firm in *Bulgaria* in order to expand further to the European market. The company, after the acquisition, decided to send an expatriate (a very experienced IT consultant) to Bulgaria to act as the temporary general director in order to guide the local staff in the newly acquired firm and transmit some core cultural values of the parent company. After a month, the expatriate decided to introduce 3 major organizational changes in order to improve the performance of the acquired firm. In particular:

- He introduced individual performance-related pay with a bonus and benefits based on several quantitative criteria (e.g. the number of contracts with clients, etc.) for all employees.
- He enhanced workforce flexibility by making IT designers work from home 2 days a week.
- He gave extensive job autonomy and decision-making power to the junior technical staff (i.e. IT designers).

However, after 6 months, an employee satisfaction survey revealed that the vast majority of Bulgarian workers were unhappy with the overall working climate and that they had reduced motivation.

Task

Using relevant theory, discuss the cross-cultural issues that the expatriate faced in relation to the management of the new teams of employees in Bulgaria and provide suggestions on what the expatriate can do to overcome those problems and boost staff motivation. What do you think is the role of *employee learning*, and how can it be stimulated in the specific company?

Key points of the chapter

Nowadays, an increasing number of small organizations decide to engage in international business activities to survive and boost their profitability. However, the international business arena is full of challenges since the external (macro) environment becomes complicated. It is therefore crucial for small firm owners to acquire an in-depth knowledge of cross-cultural management to understand how culture shapes employee behaviour at work and how it impacts individual learning.

Hofstede's cultural framework provides a useful tool for the analysis of cultural differences among countries. The model outlines the impact of culture on employee behaviour using several dimensions. National culture does affect the nature and extent of employee learning in small organizations. People from different cultural backgrounds learn in different ways and interpret information based on their cultural beliefs. Hence, all small firm owners that engage in international business activities should be aware of the impact of different cultural values on skills development if they are to design effective learning activities that can enhance employee knowledge.

References

Hofstede, G. (1980) *Culture's consequences: international differences in work related values.* Beverly Hills: Sage Publications.

Kolb, D. A. (1984) *Experiential learning: experience as the source of learning and development.* NJHoboken: Prentice Hall Publications.

Conclusion

This publication has attempted to fill the knowledge gap in relation to the ways employees in small enterprises learn and acquire new skills, which are considered the basis of organizational success at national and international levels. The analysis pointed to the value of small firms adopting a high-skills business strategy. Several research studies in the wider fields of small business management and HRM have stressed the need for small organizations in several sectors of economic activity to abandon their cost-minimization approaches to profitability and shift their strategies towards high-value-added production in order to remain competitive in domestic and foreign markets.

In several countries across the globe, policy makers attempt to support such a high-skills strategy by increasing the supply of skills in the labour market, mainly in the form of an expanded formal education system and training subsidies. However, such a narrow policy intervention neglects other significant areas required to support a 'high-skills' strategy, such as an array of macroeconomic policies and changes in the workplace. A central message of this publication is that the answers to such questions depend on a complex of factors influencing the skill intensity of the production process and that the significance of employer demand for more and higher skills should be recognized. Boosting qualification levels of the available workforce will not, itself, produce the kind of economic benefits that policy makers desire. The key issue is to ensure that skills once created get used to productive effect within firms.

A key message from this study is that while a high-skills route to industrial development may be feasible, achieving it requires care in building appropriate institutional conditions and in ensuring that employers demand such skills. In simple terms, the importance of employer demand for a well-educated workforce cannot be over-emphasized. Small firm owner commitment towards the achievement of a high-skills society and the key role of informal learning for workforce skills development are two core factors that should be acknowledged in any discussion around HRD in the small business context. Skill policies need to embrace a much

DOI: 10.4324/9781003381815-8

broader range of 'demand-side' interventions capable of changing the way firms compete, design jobs and manage their employees if substantive progress is to be achieved. Such interventions should involve high-trust HRM systems, which encourage new forms of work organization and job design (i.e. a significant reduction in unskilled/low-skilled jobs) and the spread of coaching networks that facilitate the informal learning activities of small firms.

Furthermore, policy makers have considered formal learning a major target area for public intervention claiming that formal learning constitutes the most important way of acquiring and developing the skills and competencies required at work. Yet, they appear to lack the required flexibility and relevance to attract small firm owners' interest. The analysis in this effort reveals that small firms do not want, require or need formal systems of training (e.g. off-the-job training). Even in those firms where a more highly skilled workforce is demanded, research evidence shows that informal learning features as their preferred method of skills development. In particular, the findings from several empirical studies indicate that small firm owners favour employee development approaches that emphasize experiential, informal and self-directed learning, thus facilitating organizational development. Learning from other people and the challenge of the work itself prove to be the most important dimensions of learning in the small business context.

It should be recognized that learning within small firms is often informal and incidental and facilitated by managers/supervisors and peers (i.e. employees learn from their everyday experiences in informal ways). Unless policy makers and firm owners engage with the issue of informal learning and understand exactly how such informal practices can be harnessed in more sophisticated ways to push small enterprises towards more high skills agendas, skill development policies will be doomed to failure.

The study also brings fresh thought around the impact of informal learning on small firm competitiveness by revealing that it can be a key factor for improved organizational performance. The prevailing wisdom on HRD in small firms is that not much is done: The evidence is that such firms do not spend equivalent on training compared to large companies and rarely have a staff member with a dedicated training role. Hence, it is often assumed their HRD is inferior, if not non-existent. However, the present study reveals a high degree of unplanned and informal learning activity in small firms, which simply cannot be measured by means of indicators traditionally used in the field of education and training, such as participation rates, training hours, expenditures or level of qualification. One of the key messages of this research effort is that an absence of formal training does not mean that small firms do not train *per se*. They do train and it should be acknowledged that informal learning is not an inferior form of learning. It is fundamental, necessary and valuable in its own right as it helps small firms to meet skill shortage needs, reduce errors during the production process, introduce sophisticated technology, respond to changes and increase job satisfaction for workers. This is not to suggest that such forms of learning automatically relate to improved firm performance but to suggest that understanding the processes by which informal learning practices are stimulated, developed and implemented in small firms, and how such practices link to wider firm strategy and HRM context, is necessary if academics and practitioners are to understand how to stimulate skills upgrading and skills demand in such firms.

Another key concluding point of this effort is that the contribution of learning is not limited to economic terms. It should be recognized that employee learning does offer various social benefits as well. For example, it has a vital role to play in combating in-work poverty. The present effort revealed that employee learning can help the working poor improve their living conditions. This means that staff development is closely linked to corporate citizenship.

A concluding point of this publication is that HRM synergy is critical for skills development in the small business context. As the discussion in Chapter 4 revealed, the process of informal learning is severely affected by other core HR activities including staff selection, performance appraisal and rewards. Small firm owners should place equal emphasis on all the major HR activities if they are to evolve into learning organizations. All the HR functions are heavily interlinked with each other, so a change in just one HR element will not bring the desired performance improvement outcomes. Organizations need to make improvements in all the HR areas (e.g. proper HR planning, rigorous staff selection, regular performance evaluations, generous performance-related rewards, etc.) in order to achieve superior performance.

Index

Printed in the United States
by Baker & Taylor Publisher Services

Printed in the United States
by Baker & Taylor Publisher Services